ETHNIC CONFLICT IN CENTRAL ASIA

ETHNIC CONFLICT IN CENTRAL ASIA

A Comparative Study of Tibet and Kazakhstan

By

Dr. P. Geetha Lakshmi Ph.D.

Cosmo Publications

2003 New Delhi

ETHNIC CONFLICT IN CENTRAL ASIA

First COSMO Print 2003

ISBN 81-7755-552-9

Published by

MRS. RANI KAPOOR
for COSMO PUBLICATIONS Div. of
GENESIS PUBLISHING PVT. LTD.
24-B, Ansari Road, Darya Ganj,
New Delhi-110 002, INDIA
Ph.: 2327 8779, 2328 0455
Fax : 2324 1200

Composed at

Cosmo Publications

Printed at

Mehra Offset Press

Contents

ACKNOWLEDGEMENT

My thanks are due to the omniscient and omnipresent *God*, in different forms, who stood by me to complete this seemingly endless task successfully.

I express my deepest regards and sincere gratitude to my supervisor Dr. Dawa Norbu, Associate professor Central Asian Studies Division, School of International Studies. His valuable suggestions put me on the right track. He has been a friend philosopher and guide.

I am extremely grateful To Dr. B.D. Ghoshal, Chairperson, CSCSEASWPS, Prof. Kalim Bahadur, Prof. B. D. Arora and other Professors of the Centre for their co-operations. My thanks are due to Dr. K. Warikoo for creating interest on ethnic conflict in this region. I had the fortune of meeting Mr. Z. Kaliev, Mr. Z.M. Abdilidin and Ms. L.A. Baishina of Kazakhstan at International Seminar on India Central Asia in December 1995. Prof. Keith Pratt, of Department of East Asian Studies University of Durrham, England happened to be in India during the final stages of my research work. Prof. Ram Rahul and Prof. V.C. Bhutani encouraged me to deal with this challenging topic. My discussions with all of them and their critical comments generated new insights and enriched my work. Correspondence with Dr. Michael Dillion, University of Durrhum, has been of great help. The affectionate ways and best wishes of Dr. Ganganth Jha and Dr. Klaus Sagaster (Germany) inspired me constantly.

I was blessed with the sacred presence of His Holiness the Dalai Lama, in October 1995.

I am extremely grateful to Dr. Anand Kumar, Indo-

Tibet Friendship Society. Mrs. Tsening Norzom Thonsu, President, Tibetan Women's Association (Dharamsala) and all India Student Forum for Free Tibet for providing access to latest reports and materials.

My pranams are due to my parents, and unstinting support. At trying times, the constant encouragement of my uncles and aunts, brothers—Rama Krishna, Padma Vadina, Chaitanya and Anantna Krishan, boosted my confidence. I am also thankful to my cousins Suryanarayana and Jaysree for their love and affection

My friends, Ms. K. Savitri, teaching political science in Jamia Milia University; Anita, Lakshmi, Sujatha, Manila, Prem Lata, Vijya Lakshmi, Smitha, Vyjayanti, Rajitha, K.S. Reddy, Ramesh, Siddoji, Chinnayya, Kishore, Santosh and Poorna Mohanty—research scholars in JNU, deviated from their busy academic schedule to extend their help in all possible ways.

I am thankful to ICSSR for giving me financial assistance at the right time.

I am also thankful to the library staff of Institute for Defence Studies and Analysis (IDSA), Indian Council for World Affairs, Nehru Memorial Museum and Library, American Centre Library, India International Centre Library, Ratan Tata Library, Department of Chinese and Japanese Studies, (Delhi University), Bureau of H.H. Dalai Lama, U.N. Information Centre, Human Rights Documentation Centre and JNU Library.

The Staff of Ganga Mess also need special mention. They took care of me throughout my stay at the University because of my restricted food habits.

I express my infinite love and affection to my husband, Satya Saibabu. He has been supportive of this work that has taken many years which could have been meaningfully spent with him. His rational thinking kept my interest alive and made the earliest completion of this work—a dream come true. Though we were physically apart he has been spiritually with me throughout the course of this study. This work is much his as is mine.

My gratitude to all the above mentioned is beyond words.

P. GEETHA LAKSHMI

PREFACE

Ethnicity is not a structure or an entry, it is a process-peel.

The study of ethnic conflict in multi-national communist states especially in the context of world-wide upsurge in assertion of ethnic identities and cultural symbols, is timely but challenging. The persistence of ethnicity and its various manifestations—religious, cultural and linguistic—in recent years, have shaped the events in may communist states. The Central Asian region, with the Tibetan and Kazakh ethnic minorities in the Chinese and erstwhile Soviet territories, is a special case for study. Central Asia's peculiarities, particularly, its strategic location, history and the ongoing socio-economic process are important determinants of the overall ethnic situation in this region.

A comparative analysis of ethnic conflict in Tibet and Kazakhstn is of great significance since these two regions experienced more or less similar forms of domination under the hegemony of the two communist giants—China and the Soviet Union respectively. The policies of nationalities in these two regions were based on Marxist ideology and originally formulated by Lenin. China followed Soviet line for a brief period. Later, Mao attempted to revise it to suit, 'Chinese characteristics'. However, both China and the Soviet Union aimed at assimilation and integration of various ethnic minorities into a single whole. In the process, minority cultures and languages were ridiculed and destroyed. Tibetans suffered greater losses than Kazakhs under communist rule. Despite this, their deep attachment to ethnic factors religion, language and culture—has not lessened. Communist reforms helped Tibetans and Kazakhs to improve their standard of living. The reform programmes aimed at modernization (tantamount to Signification and Russification respectively) perpetuated inequalities. Domination of Chines and Russina in Key areas of economic life caused resentment. The loosening of controls with the advent of Deng's four modernization processes and Gorbachev's Persetroika and Glasnost, both aimed at changes in economic or political life of these two countries had ethnic consequences. Anti- Chines and anti Russian feeling were more openly expressed A series of ethnic demonstrations and disturbances occurred in both the case, dating dramatieally since 1986-87.

The present study is a humble attempt to compare the ethnic conflict in Tibet and Kazakhstan, the two significant cases in Central Asia. The period chosen for this purpose is 1986-1991. The largest demonstration (after 1959) in 1987 in Lhasa and the first ethnic disturbance in Alma-Ata in late 1986 dragged the attention of scholars to this region once again. At this juncture, major economic reforms were on in Tibet. In Kazakhstan, only a year and a half passed since Gorbachev's accession to power. The events in the most Russified and least Islamised part of Soviet Central Asia, soft underbelly of the Soviet Union, was major shock to Moscow. More than that, the repercussions, of these events, which brought the whole country under ethnic turmoil in no time, led to re-thinking on 'Nationality Quton which was initially neglected by Gorbachev. The demonstrations in Tibet did not have such intensity. Except for Xinjiang, anti-Chinese moves did not occur in other parts of China. Thus, inspite of certain similarities in the nature, causes, and consequences of ethnic conflicts, they did not yield similar results. The study aims to compare and contrast these two cases ethnic conflict and explain why such similar policies led to different out comes.

During the course of my research, despite the paucity of primary sources the abundance of secondary sources available, in their latest and revised editions made this subject ever-interesting and more demanding. I have used no standard way of transliterating Chinese. Tibetan, Russian and Kazakh names. I have used same spellings used by different authors differently on the subject. For example, Srong-Tsan-Gampo is also spelled Song-bstan-bsgampo. I have tried my level best to pool all source available in India to understand this dynamic topic and present a comprehensive analysis of the problem in a comparative perspective. Major merits, if there are any, in this kind of academic exercise, they are (a) comparative analysis, and (b) ethnic conflict, both of which are in the need of redefining and refining through this academic practice.

1

Introduction

Ethnicity is an important determinant of socio-political realities of multi-ethnic states in post-colonial world. The interplay of history and the forces of modernity have stimulated individualization and added a powerful new meaning and force to the local cultures, religions and languages which act as key elements in defining one's ethnic identity. Over the years ethnic conflict has become a major manifestation of post-colonial nationalism.

The focus of the proposed study is ethnic conflict in strategically located Central Asia. The study deals with the two cases of ethnic conflict, Kazakhstan (Soviet Central Asia) and Tibet (Chinese Central Asia), from a comparative perspective. Kazakhstan is the largest among Soviet Central Asian Republics (now CIS). Under Tsarist rule it had traumatic experiences. The colonization of the Kazahk Steppe led to expulsion of Kazakhs from the best grazing lands and prevention from pursuing their traditional mode of life-nomadism. Exodus of foreigners resulted in economic hardships and decline in living standards. Conflicts between natives and foreigners became a special feature of the steppe life.

Unlike Kazakhstan, Tibet had all the features of an independent nation in the pre-communist era. Looking at the

Sino-Tibetan relations in historical perspective, it is abundantly clear that till the end of the seventeenth century the relations between the two nations were based on equality and mutual dependence. At times of crisis China gave military aid. Many wars during the nineteenth century were fought and settled by the Tibetans themselves. It was a self-sufficient society founded on Buddhist faith. The Dalai Lama was the spiritual and political leader of Tibet. Even today Tibetans consider Dalai Lama as personification of Tibetan national identity. Besides, Tibet has had most of the attributes of a nationality: language, culture, religion, history, political institutions different from Hama China.

After the Bolshevik Revolution, the nationalities were expected to join the Soviet Union voluntarily. Special declarations were made to attract the Muslim minorities of Central Asia. The development of their home lands and cultures was assured. Though there were protests, the Soviet regime suppressed them and incorporated the Muslim minorities into the Soviet orbit. By 1936 Kazakhstan was elevated to the status of Union Republic. The very creation of republic provided Kazakhs with distinct territorial framework wherein they could develop their ethnic identities. However, in practice, an intensive reform campaign had dramatically changed the over all socio-economic situation. All these reforms aimed at creating new Soviet people; Russians were deported to help the modernizing process. The increasing presence of Russians reduced the Kazakhs to a minority in their own republic. Kazakh history has deep roots in Islamic culture and tradition and customs. Soviet policies were targeted at Islamic ways of life. Atheistic propaganda was launched. Besides this, Kazakhs were discriminated vis-a-vis Russians in all spheres of public life. Top party positions and administrative posts were manned by the Russians. All these processes of Sovietisation or Russification kindled the latent ethnic awareness of Kazakhs, Gorbachev's liberalizing policies -*Perestroika* and *glasnost*—gave vent to the suppresed feelings. The first outburst of nationalist sentiments was reported in Alma-Ata, Kazakh capital, which triggered a nationalist chain reaction throughout the country since then.

Once a colony, Kazakhstan became a republic under Soviet rule. Contrary to this, once independent country Tibet became an Autonomous Region of China. As a result of colonization of free Tibet in the present age of decolonization, the Tibetans suffered in human treatment. The sudden and violent occupation of Tibet by the People's Liberation Army distorted the status quo of Tibet. Since Chinese Communists, unlike Bolshevik leaders, did not expect the minorities to join China willingly, PLA was entrusted with the task of bringing minority areas under Chinese control.

Chinese exodus similar to Russian exodus, reduced Tibetans to minority status in their own land. Chinese economic exploitation of Tibet includes large-scale forced labour, collectivization, confiscation of ancient wealth. Following soviet model Chinese authorities launched major offensive against Buddhism, the predominant religion of the Tibetan masses. Chinese dominated important spheres of social and political life of Tibetans which led to discontent. After nine years of Chinese occupation unprecedented nationalist demonstrations were held in 1959. After the Cultural Revolution China's Tibet policy was revised. Later Deng's modernization processes lifted the hegemonic controls to some extent and initiated liberalization process. Once again more demonstrations dragged the attention of press in 1987 and 1989. The later events may be understood in the light of ethnic turmoil in neighbouring Soviet Central Asia.

The issue of minorities better known as 'National Question' in Marxist writings has been a thorny issue for the two great communist regimes of the world, the Soviet Union and China.

The principle of national self-determination was basic to the Soviet Nationalities policy. This right to self-determination is enshrined in the Soviet Constitution. It gives nationalities, the right to secede from the Union. According to the principles of Chinese National Minority policies the right to self-determination implies 'each nation has a right to constitute an independent state and determine its own government'. As Marxist-Leninists, the Chinese agreed whole heartedly that the right to secession applied only to colonial cases and the principle of self-determination in a socialist context meant only 'self-government' or 'autonomy'. They however, differed on the question of self-government; while the Soviets adopted a federalist framework China opted for a unitary state with regional autonomy.

While Kazakhstan was accorded the status of a Union Republic, Tibet was given only regional autonomy. It is because China claimed Tibet as an integral part of China for centuries and treated Tibetans on par with other minorities (Mongols; Manchus, Turks) Tibet became an autonomous region of China. The national minorities policies of Soviet Union and China aimed at assimilation and integration through the so-called democratic and liberalized reforms. Both talked about new union of man during the revolutionary period. Ironically they ended up in imposing the language and culture of the dominant group on reluctant minorities. These processes and policies had a humiliating implication to the minorities ethnic identity. But official sources went on portraying a picture of harmony and unions of all nationalities-Russians or the Chinese as the case may be.

In retrospect, the Soviet and Chinese policies proved to be counter-productive. Ethnic awareness, identification with language, culture, religion which differ from those of majority has been on the rise; ethno-religious and cultural revivalism strengthened ethnic ties. Movements for nationalism, whose goal is independence, were launched in both countries by 1980s. But the authorities labelled them as parochial, tribal, sub-national, counter-revolutionary, anti-national, separatist etc.

In the last decade Kazakhstan and Tibet witnessed violent ethnic turmoil. Though the first anti-Chinese demonstration was held in Tibet as early as 1959, the demonstrations of 1987 and 1989 were given more press attention. All these events took place in Lhasa. In Kazakhstan immediately after a year of Perestroika ethnic riots took place in the capital Aima-Ata. Another major disturbance occurred in 1989 in Novy Uzen.

Ethno-religious revivalism took place. Islam and Buddhism both contained a high tradition of great scholarly sophistication, which constituted the banner of political and spiritual reform and revival within their respective societies. Besides religion, language and culture were also revived. Though few factors are common to both Kazakhstan and Tibet in arousing ethnic conflict, the outcomes in the two cases are different and, one of the purposes of this thesis is to explain why this is so.

After a series of ethnic conflicts in Soviet Central Asia and throughout the Soviet Union, ethnic nationalism reached its epitome. Gradually the various republics announced declarations of independence. Kazakhstan proclaimed its sovereignty in November, 1991. Among the fifteen republics eleven formed Commonwealth of Independent States. Thus Kazakhstan stands as independent today.

As a for as Tibet is concerned, among the minority nationalities it was only Tibetans who were more expressive in their demands for independence. They lacked support either from other minorities inside China or from independent states of the world. Though some countries have paid lip service to Tibetan cause, they failed to stand by their words at international for a.

Moreover, Tibet is first an autonomous region unlike Kazakhstan which was a republic. The level of socio-economic development of Tibet is far lesser when compared to Kazakhstan. The more powerful China made Tibet its army camp. Above all, China in the 1980s did not face system wide legitimation crisis, unlike the former Soviet Union.

With this general background this study aims to compare the two situations of ethnic conflicts and explains why it led to different outcomes in both the cases under study.

Theoretical Concepts and Approaches

Multi-ethnic states face greater intensity of cleavages within the social order as well as between society and the state. These states are divided not only by economic interests, but also by racial, religious and cultural factors to a much greater extent than non-multi-ethnic states. This is particularly so because colonial rule/majority rule exacerbated rather than diminished existing divisions. Hence the problem of accommodating protest and integrating divisive groups became much greater. The issue here is bringing minorities and political apparatus into a satisfactory relationship in a process of modernising traditional social orders (Tibet) and democratizing the political culture (Kazakhstan). The following theoretical approaches are of great help in understanding ethnic conflict in Central Asia.

Simpson and Yinger (1992) have identified six basic patterns of ethnic and racial relations and conflict which range from a pattern of co-existence to a pattern of continuing, hostile conflict. Briefly stated, these patterns are, (1) assimilation (2) pluralism (3) legal protection of minorities (4) population transfer (5) continued subjugation and (6) extermination. Among these (1), (3) and (4) may be observed in both the cases—Tibet and Kazakhstan. While continued subjugation is applicable to Tibetans only, pluralism, (existence of many ethnic groups) may be realized in Kazakhstan. Various studies of these patterns in different societies point to atleast, three causal factors being present in situations of ethnic and racial conflict. They may be summarized as follows.

1. The existence of two or more social groups with distinct and easily identifiable physical (Tibetan and Chinese) characteristics or very distinctive cultural and social practices (Tibetans vs Chinese and Kazakhs vs Russians).

2. The existence of competition between these social groups, marked by distinctive physical features or cultural and social practices, for access to and control of scarce resources. (*e.g.* land, water, jobs, political power etc).

   This factor may be understood in the context of both Tibetans and Kazakhs in the following chapters. Similar argument is made by Brass (1990).

3. These social groups must be unequal in their powers so that one group is capable of enforcing claims to scarce physical, cultural or social resources at the direct expense of the other group or groups.

The participants in ethnic conflict fight not only about the details of history, but also of rules as applied to them of laws from which they should be exempt, of particular rights which they have been deprived, of special status they should enjoy, the details of past injustices and of future guarantees (John Chipman). These trends are observed in both the cases under study.

Perhaps the biggest surprise for students of ethnic relations in recent years has been the sudden upsurge of ethnic nationalism in Communist states, especially the Soviet bloc. Within the Soviet Union Kazakhstan witnessed the first out burst of ethnonational sentiments and paved the way for further ethnic crisis in the country as a whole. In the space of few years, nationalist movements arose in several areas. The resultant ethnic violence ultimately led to unthinkable consequences. All this seems incompatible with the philosophy and practice of Communism, in which nationalism is supposed to disappear, to be replaced by patriotism and 'Proletarian internationalism' (Connor 1984).

Ideology remains a central feature of Chinese rule in Tibet. Tibetan's protest for the restoration of nationhood is overtly political, targeting the Chinese state and apparatus of the social control that maintains state power (PLA). Under these conditions Tibetans assert themselves to be a nation and define themselves in political terms. The definition of nationalism as "a theory of political legitimacy, which requires that ethnic boundaries should not cut across political ones[1] must be qualified to reflect the Tibetan experience of the Communist state.

Methology

With the rising critiques of positivist methods comparative research is in vogue which broadens the scholar's view point. There is a lake of understanding about comparative analysis and therefore the concept of comparative analysis should be stated here briefly. Comparative study means that we study one general problem (ethnic conflict) under different historical situations which constitutes points of comparison and contrast. Thus, Barringtion Moore, in his *Social Origins of Democracy and Dictatorship,* takes up the problem of democracy and dictatorship emerging under different historical conditions in USA, England, Germany, France, China and India. We know there is not much similarity in the historical background of most of these countries mentioned above. The task of Comparative Analysis is how a general problem is handled differently/similarly under different/similar conditions. In this sense comparative analysis is similar to physical science experiments in which an element or compound is put under different conditions like

1. E.Gellener, *Nations and Nationalism* (Oxford, Basil Blackwell, 1983), p.1.

temperature and pressure. In social sciences we can't do controlled experiments, that is why we do comparative analysis. Our general problem in this thesis is Ethnic Conflict and the two sets of conditions under which ethnic conflict takes place are those of Tibet and Kazakhstan. This will enable us to find out why Kazakhstan became independent and Tibet did not, even though ethnic conflict is taking place in both the countries.

There are points of similarities (communist takeover, discriminating policies, dominant role of tradition) both actually and functionally as well as dissimilarities, Such as, differences in communist political structures, policies, cultural orientations (Islamic/Buddhist) etc. A comparative study must contend with the fact that the same process (modernization/ assimilation) from the point of view of sociological analysis takes on different names (Great Leap Forward Cultural Revolution in China and Virgin Lands Scheme, Atheistic Propaganda in the Soviet Union).

Therefore, the methodology for this study is basically comparative analysis of a single problem i.e ethnic conflict in two different/ similar conditions Tibet and Kazakhstan. We will employ concepts and methods from comparative studies, sociology, and political science. But the main body of the study will be historical analysis of Ethnic Conflict, refinement of ethnic conflict concepts and ethnic identity, as the two cases are rich in Islamic and Buddhist cultural identities. The essence of comparative inquiry is that 'comparables' be compared. Simply put, the units of comparison must be sufficiently similar to make comparison feasible as well as sufficiently different to make it fruitful (Alexander J. Motyl; 1989), as is the case here. To conclude, comparative nationality studies are ideal for evaluating existing theories-theories of ethnic conflict, of centre-periphery relations etc.

In the following pages, chapter II deals with Policies towards Nationalities in the Soviet Union and China. It focuses on to aspects-'domination' and 'assimilation'. The implications of these policies are critically analysed. Differences and similarities in the two policies (Chinese and Soviet) are also discussed.

Chapter III covers, Communist Reforms since 1986 i.e., the developments of the last decade. The impact of liberalization on the ethnic trends in China and the USSR in the context of Gorbachev's *Perestroika* and *glasnost* and Deng Xiaoping's four modernization measures are examined here.

Chapter IV describes ethnic identities in Tibet and Kazakhstan focussing on factors that perpetuate ethnicity race, language, religion and culture. It attempted to explain how these factors strengthened ethnic ties and aroused nationalistic feelings. It is shown that although ethnic identities are functionally similar, subjectively and objectively they exist in different forms Buddhist or Islamic, Tibetan or Kazakh etc.

Chapter V narrates the ethnic conflict in Tibet and Kazakhstan in 1980s expecially in Lhasa in Tibet and Alma-Ata and Novy-Uzen in Kazakhstan. This chapter, compares and contrasts the two cases of ethnic conflict under different/similar conditions and highlights those factors which played a crucial role in intensifying inter-ethnic tensions in each case. Special emphasis is given to ethnic mobilization strategies.

In Chapter VI, it is explained Why Kazakhstan became independent and Tibet did not. It analyses the constitutional statuses of the two entities and its impact on the overall development. It also explains how various factors—demographic imbalance, quality of ethnic mobilization, the extent to which the dominant ethnic group has control over the state apparatus, and the international factor led to different outcomes in the two cases.

The concluding chapter will summarize the major findings of this comparative study of ethnic conflict in Central Asia.

2

Policies Towards Nationalities in China and Soviet Union

In a multi-national country, the state formulates its policies towards nationalities in such a way that the outcome—integration of all nationalities into a single whole—is often taken for granted. But the dynamic behaviour of nationalities ethnic groups over the years has proved that various policies of assimilation and integration are counter-productive. In communist societies of post-colonial world the 'nationality question' has become a serious concern of policy-makers. Their ability to appease minority ethnic groups decides the territorial integrity of multi-ethnic states.

This chapter will examine the nature, content, and practice of nationality policies in China and the former Soviet Union. Towards the end a comparison of both the situations will be made.

Composition and Distribution of Ethnic Groups in China

In China, besides the Han people, there exist 55 different nationalities. They are Mongols, Hui, Tibetan, Uighur, Miao, Yi, Chuang, Pu-yi Korean, Manchu, Kazakh, T'ung, Pai (Min—Chia), T'ai K'awa, Ha-ni, Yao, Li, T'u-chia, Tung-hsiang, Kirghiz,T'u

Li-su Nung, Na-hsi, La-hu, Shu-chia, Ching-po', Ch'iang, Kao-shan, Tatar, Russian, Uzbek, Tajik, Pao-an, Yu-ku, Salar, Sibo, Olunch'un, and several tens of other nationalities.[1] While the Han nationalities comprise 92 percent of the population, non-Han minorities mentioned above constitute the remaining eight per cent of the population numbering over 91 million people and occupy 65 per cent of the total Chinese territory.[2] There is enormous diversity among these nationalities. The Chuang is the largest among them, numbering some 13 million, while the Olunch'un with a population of about, 2,000 is the smallest. These minority nationalities intermingle with the Han and with each other to a very large extent and form small compact communities of different sizes.

The distribution of China's national minorities form a very complicated pattern. Hans occupied fertile agricultural lands and industrialized regions with high population density. Non-Han people settled on steppes, desert oases or steep mountains and border lands supporting themselves by pastoralism, shifting cultivation or other special adaptations to their environment.[3] In some of the minority areas, such as Inner Mongolia, Guangxi, Ningxia, etc. the Han nationality is a majority, accounting for more than 60 to 80 per cent of the population. The Hui nationality numbers about 7.2 million, of which only a little more than a million live in the Ningxia Hui Autonomous Region: the rest are found all over the country. About one million Tibetans out of a total of 3.8 million (according to the 1982 census) are found in the Tibetan Autonomous Region: the others live in Gansu, Qinghhai, Sichuan, Yunnan, etc. The Uyghur nationality is most extensively found in Xinjiang Uygur Autonomous Region, but large numbers of 11 other minorities and the Han nationality live together.[4]

This complicated distribution pattern of nationalities in China is the historical result of large-scale ethnic shifts due to needs in production and daily life, mutual exchanges, wars, natural calamities, regional separatist rule, etc. Today, these minority peoples live in the most sensitive areas, making their loyalty, from Beijing's perspective, a crucial element in maintaining China's territorial integrity.[5]

Policy towards Minority Nationalities before 1949

In the Confucian tradition, China's ethnic minorities and neighbouring, peoples have been regarded as 'barbarians' of one kind or another. The Han policies aimed to control them through a combination of conquest and assimilation. The downfall of Qing dynasty in 1911 heralded a post-imperial era for China. The new government adopted a new national flag consisting of five horizontal bars in different colours. Each colour was to symbolise the five 'races' of China; the Hans, Manchus, Mongols, Tibetans, and the Tatars (a term for the various Turkic-speaking peoples). This division reflected the relative prominence of these ethnic groups during the Quing dynasty rather than any conscious theory of the ethnic composition of China.

Sun Yat-sen, father of 'Chinese Nationalism' was of the opinion that the Chinese state for all practical purposes consisted of one nationality. Later, under the influence of Comintern agents, working with the Guomindang (Kuomintang) (GMD) the concepts of self-determination and autonomy for minorities were formulated as part of GMD policy.

The pre-1949 policy of the Chinese Communist Party (CCP which was formed in 1921) concerning the minorities may—like the overall CCP political strategy for the liberation of China—be divided into a pre-1935 and post-1935 period, i.e. before and after the ascent of Mao zedong (Mao-Tse-tung) as supreme leader of CCP and before after the Long March.[6] In its earliest years CCP appears to have accepted unquestionably

Marxist-Soviet pronouncements on minorities with little regard to how they should be adopted to the Chinese situation. As early as at the Second Congress of CCP in 1922, the Manifesto of the Congress proposed that China proper (including Manchuria, the present Northeast), was to be a true democratic republic and that the three regions of Mongolia, Tibet, and Turkestan (present day Xinjiang) were to be autonomous, forming democratic, self-governing regions. China, Mongolia, Tibet and Turkestan would unite on the basis of their own free will, thereby establishing a Chinese federal republic[7]. Another important event was the 'Draft Constitution' promulgated by the First Soviet Congress in November 1931. It contained resolution concerning policy towards nationalities, including the fundamental rules for national self-determination.[8] It stated, "All Mongolians, Tibetans, Miao, Yao, Koreans, and others living on the territory of China shall enjoy the full right to self-determination, i.e., they may either join the Union of Chinese Soviets or secede from it and form their own state as they may prefer."[9] This statement seemed to illustrate the fact that communists were more democratic than the nationalists.

The CCP's position in the post 1931 period on the right of self-determination marked a distinct departure both from its past policy and from Lenin's stand. This change can be attributed to the experience during the Long March. The notion of self-determination was replaced by "national regional autonomy." Mao was held responsible for the new line in China's national minorities policy as it emerged at the time when he rose to power within the leadership of the CCP.[10] Mao seemed to argue that the answer to the national minorities problem was neither independence nor autonomy per se. Instead, the free union of nationalities shall replace national oppression and even that was possible under the Soviets.[11] This idea of Mao seems to have a bearing on Chinese communist thinking till date.

In the true Marxist-Leninist sense, Mao, believed that the national question was product of inequality and oppression, and would automatically be resolved once socialism is established in China. The goal of CCP was accordingly, to end the inequality between the ethnic groups through a programme of gradual, cultural, economic and political equality. In the light of the above views expressed by Mao, it is imperative that one analyses the various phases of minorities polices since 1949.

Minority Policies during early years of People's Republic of China

When the Communists came to power in 1949, they sent People;s Liberation Army (PLA),to include the border regions to the Chinese territory, since there was persistent resistance to Han-Communist rule in those areas. Chinese leaders attempted to win the loyalty or atleast, the acquiescence of the minority peoples. At various points in China's post-revolutionary history minority policy has included the following:

(a) a combination of formal political and legal equality;

(b) active efforts to incorporate minorities into the national, political and economic system;

(c) the establishment of special ethnic administrative regions where minority languages may be used;

(d) national policies modified to suit local conditions;

(e) provision of subsidized benefits in public health, education, and economic development.[12]

The pre-1949 policies were formulated when the communist controlled very few non-Han areas. After 1949 their views underwent a transformation. The definition of autonomy was narrowed to a policy that combined Marxist ideology and Leninist-Stalinist practice with party's own experiences in dealing with China's ethnic groups. Ideologically Mao-zedong remained impeccably Marxist, stating that: the Chinese Communist Party has consistently recognized the nationalist question as being a part of the liberation of the Chinese.. what has been called nationality struggle is in reality a question of class struggle.[13]

With Mao's unchallenged authority and all group;s loyalty, any latent tensions among nationalities were kept under check. Despite some lapses, Mao chose to observe the principle of minority rights, whereby dissenters within the leadership could retain their views and even reiterate than at a later date without fear of punishment.

In the initial phase, Mao and his loyalists followed a policy of gradualism and pluralism. Minority customs and habits were tolerated in regions inhabited by minorities. Minority elites of feudal origin became political leaders. The concept and practices of class struggle, so prevalent in other parts of China, were purposefully muted when applied to minority regions.[14] The 1949 Constitution promised protection of national customs and special cultural features as also unequivocal guarantee of linguistic freedom (Article 77).

Various constitutional provisions were clearly at variance with an ideology that interpreted nationality differences as class differences and aimed at wiping them out as soon as possible. With the prospect of withering away of minority group characteristics, Marxist ideology was reinforced by Han Chinese cultural chauvinism.[15] In general, however, policy during the 1949-56 period, aimed at the conscientious implementation of the protections guaranteed in the constitution.[16]

The Party's United Front Work Department co-ordinated activities with the upper strata of the minorities groups, as well as with selected warlords, religious leaders, members of the bourgeoisie, and overseas Chinese. Within the government, the job of nationalities was handled by the state council's Nationalities Affairs Commission, and the National People's Congress which contained a Nationalities Committee. There was a greater degree of tolerance towards various issues of nationalities and there were pledges to protect their rights. Large-scale studies of the social formations, the social history, and the languages of the various minorities were launched.

Autonomous political entities were created and were organized at three levels—as regions (qu), as prefectures (Zhou), and the Counties (Xian/Qi).The majority of them were established by 1958, but the process is still going on today in the form of local adjustments. At present, there are five autonomous regions, 30 autonomous prefectures and 124 autonomous counties.[17] These regions account for about 64 per cent of China's total territory; 78 per cent of China's total minority population live in such autonomous areas.[18]

In the mid -50s, however, there were indications that themoderate, gradualist approach was not having the desired effect. In connection with a routine investigation of minorities policy and again in 1957 as part of the "hundred flowers" campaign in which people were encouraged to voice their complaints against party and the government, the results startled the CCP leadership. The responses ranged form suggestions that minorities be given more power within the system to demands for separate independent states. To put them in a single phrase "many rights in theory, few in practice". These results proved that rather than encouraging the attrition of ethnic differences, the minority policies were reinforcing existing minority identities.

Another important phenomenon was the problem of Han chauvinism in minority areas, which was manifested in the superior attitude of Han cadres towards the minorities and a tendency towards commendism (to give commends and that must obey).[19] The Central Committee of the CCP called on the press to "Publish more articles based on specific facts to criticise Han Chauvinism openly and educate the party members and the people".[20] Therefore, a re-thinking of the party's policies on protection of minorities took place in 1956-57. Until 1957, the policies initiated in the Han area, and the minority areas had followed different courses, but after 1957, policies towards the minority areas generally became subordinated to the overall national political priorities. A campaign to eliminate Great Han Chauvinism was launched which indicated that minorities had been enjoying no real autonomy.

The Great Leap Foward

The late 1950s saw the beginning of the radical experiments of the People's Communes and the ensuing Great Leap Forward which spelled a sharp turn about in minorities policies. This period ushered in a rapid change in policies toward the national minorities. For the period from 1956 to 1968, the policy shifted from gradualism and pluralism to one of radical assimilation. Narrowing of inter-pretation of protections given to minorities occurred with the intr-oduction of massive social and economic experiment i.e. Great Leap Forward.

Born of a general mood of impatience with the pace of China's ideological and economic developments, the Great Leap Forward also included a reaction against the relevance of the Soviet model to the Chinese context. The wide range of radical reforms affected minorities as well as Han Chinese. However, propaganda guns were directed against ethnic resistance to rapid transformation which was branded 'local nationalism'. At the same time the earlier campaign against 'Han Chauvinism' diminished considerably.

The Leap also included a mass effort to improve literacy rates. But the language taught in spare-time literary schools was Han Chinese. And in ordinary schools servicing minority areas, curricular emphasis switched from patriotism and the unity of ethnic groups to education in struggle and the Marxist-Leninist view of nationalities.[21] Training of minority cadres was intensified. More importantly, socialist reforms, such as co-operatives were introduced.

These policies of assimilation resulted in tension and violent clashes, the best known one being the uprising in Lhasa, in March 1959. Anti-Communist activity spread from eastern Tibet into the central region. There was unrest in several other minority regions. In Yunnan some Dai people fled to HongKong while others attempted to create an "Emperor of Yunnan" (Long Yun, a former governor) under the slogan "Yunnan for the Yunnanese".[22]

Xinjiang region also witnessed numerous uprisings.

The 1960s

The main goal of CCP in the early1960s following the disasters of the Great Leap Forward was to re-connect the links between itself and the minority people. several "reactionary" minority leaders who had opposed the Leap reforms were rehabilitated. The government admitted that, acting on "misleading information", it had made grave mistakes in nationality areas. It urged respect for nationalities' cultures, saying that this had "always" been the party's policy. Those Han who worked in minority areas were urged to learn the languages of the area. Local nationalism was occasionally mentioned by the official press, but Han chauvinism received the brunt of criticism.[23] Now, the party stressed, the solution to the minority problem would be found only after a long period of time.[24] The CCP also reversed itself and acknowledged that "there is a natural community of interests among the members of a given national minority without reference to class". The new policies were meant to walk a middle ground between those of 1949-50 now dubbed "right deviations" (all unity, no struggle), and post-

1956 dubbed as "left deviations"(all struggle, no unity).[25] Thus the early 1960s saw a retreat from the most radical experiments of the late 1950s and the assimilation programmes were relaxed in the mid-1960s, prior to the Cultural Revolution. The policy of protection of minority rights remained in force until the onset of this event.

Still, the desire for integration of minorities into China proper led to some unifying actions. Roads, railways, and telecommunications began to inter-connect all parts of China. National propaganda campaigns encouraged patriotism for the PRC and loyalty to the CCP, stressing the historical links among the ethnic groups and the Han. Local media organs such as radio stations,news papers, and films developed programming in the local languages that emphasized a common culture that leaned heavily toward Han culture rather than that of the minorities. Local culture was gradually relegated to a second position. In minority border areas, economic integration and trade with China were stressed over traditional border trade with neighbouring countries. Standardized pinyin alphabets, were introduced.[26] During this phase China's government became much interested in exporting its version of socialism to Third World countries.

The Cultural Revolution

The Cultural Revolution brought back the radical line of assimilation for minority groups. It led to renewed emphasis on class struggle and subsequent unrest in the minority areas. Radical leaders claiming Mao's authority and aided by militant Young Red Guard groups attacked the "four olds: old ideas, customs, habits and culture, which were thought to be more prevalent in minority-inhabited areas than in Han areas.[27] Devastating losses were inflicted upon the traditional culture of the minorities, especially in Tibet. In an excess of zeal, young militants ransacked Tibetan temples and destroyed works of art—though the government soon called a halt to the destruction of these particular manifestations of old culture.[28] In Xinjiang Moslem clergymen were forced to walk through the streets with pig heads tied around their necks[29] Traditional clothing, hairstyles which differed from Han styles were criticised. Han settlement in minority areas was encouraged. Minority cadres were replaced by Han cadres. The Central Institute for Nationalities, along with institutions of higher education was closed.[30]

Minority rights were curtailed. Encouraged by their supporters in the leadership (such as Jiang Qing) Red Guards fought battles with those loyal to the leaders in minority areas. Many party authorities were purged or criticized during the Cultural Revolution for their opposition to it. In Mongolia and Xinjiang the leadership (Ulanhu and Wang) was ousted. The former leader of Tibetan Autonomous Region, Zhang Guoha, was however elected for the first time to full Central Committee membership which he retained until his death.[31] Minority economies were brought into line with that of Han China, and the ethnic cohesiveness of their areas further reduced. These years ago brought tension not only between the Hans and the minorities, but also within the minority groups themselves.

Any kind of special treatment of minorities was denounced by radicals. They felt that special treatment would lead to unacceptable consequences, termed 'national splittism': a perpetuation of feelings of separation among the ethnic groups of China that was detrimental to the unity of the socialist state.[32] The earlier concepts (United Front etc.) and institutions (United Front Work Department, Nationalities Committee, National People's Congress, autonomous areas system etc) were attacked. The person spearheading the radical scenario of subverted socialism was Liu Shaoqui, the president of PRC and second only to Mao in the country's power structure. His successor as Mao's heir apparent, Lin Biao, had been a champion of the Left.

During the years immediately following the Cultural Revolution, the harshest policies began to be moderated. Lin Biao was much praised, communes were reinstituted and were established in Tibet for the first time. State subsidies to the autonomous areas were drastically cut, as were the number of minority schools and radio broadcasts in minority languages.[33] Minority profile was low and the issue of protection of their rights was not publicly discussed.

Infact, the cultural revolution produced a mixed bag of results. Weighing all these sometimes conflicting evidences, one is led to conclude that the results of the cultural revolution did, on balance, represent a victory for the radical assimilationist position with respect to minority policy.[34] However, this was not to be the last swing of the policy pendulum.

The Post-Cultural Revolution Period (1970s)

Indications of still another shift towards gradualism began to appear in 1970s. Restrictions on religious practices and other activities that had come under violent attack gradually eased. In Tibet, for example, a vigorous purge had been underway in the spring of 1971 to eliminate those accused of 'sabotaging the unity of nationalities and using religious superstitions in a vain attempt to restore the feudal serf system[35] was brought to an abrupt end. Once again articles began appearing that referred to the "special characteristics" of the ethnic minority peoples and the need to take them into account when formulating policies. It was argued that minority areas now be "nationalist in form and socialist in content."[36]

Money was allocated to rebuild monasteries, mosques, temples and other historical buildings that were damaged during the Cultural Revolution. In January 1972, the Central Institute for Nationalities reopened after a six-year hiatus.[37] In other words, there was gradual return to the practices of 1950s. It was publicly acknowledged that many of the government's actions had been at the expense of the ethnic minorities. More minority cadres were recruited in party and government organs. Radio stations resumed or expanded programming in minority languages. The government showed renewed solicitude about providing minorities with a variety of items of both functional and ornamental importance uniquely to them.[38]

The matter of formal protection for these privileges, however remained unmentioned. Infact the 1975 Constitution gave less protection to minorities than did its predecessor. Various such contradictions were resolved. With the death of Mao in the fall of 1976 and the purge of his more extremist followers, the so-called 'Gang of Four', the purge of Lin Biao in 1971 had apparently removed but one segment of the radical leadership. The remaining radicals, headed by the Gang of Four, coexisted uneasily with their more conservative opposition. The ideological differences between radicals and conservatives reflected in the often contradictory policies being pursued in the years 1971-76.[39]

The Tenth Party Congress (1973) rehabilitated some of the high-ranking party figures why had been criticized for their handling of minority policy. Most prominent among them were Ulanfu (Mongolia) Li-Ching Ch'Wan and Teng Hsiao-Ping. The 1978 Constitution showed significant changes when compared to the 1975 version. Discrimination against any nationality is specifically forbidden, and it is stated that nationalities should help and learn from each other. The freedom to maintain languages and customs was guaranteed, as was appropriate representation in organs of autonomous government.[40]

The new leadership that emerged in the final years of the 1970s—under Deng Xiaoping, Hu Yaobang and Zhao Ziyang—pledged to implement policies that were remarkably similar to those of the 1950s. The policies of Lin Biao and the'Gang of

Four' were deemed 'feudal' and 'fascist'.[41] United Front was resumed with minority elites, both lay and clerical. In Tibet, nobility imprisoned since the 1959 revolt were released. Grass lands and barley fields were once again used for their original purposes after being used, unsuccessfully, to grow wheat during the GPCR (Great Proletariat Cultural Revolution). True regional autonomy was once touted with the admission that in the past it had degenerated into "mere formality". Religious piligrimages were once again possible.[42] Knowledge of local languages was considered essential to serve the four modernization—policies introduced by Hua-Deng government to rapidly develop China's agriculture, industry, science and technology and defence.

Latest Phase

The newest Constitution promulgated in 1982 addresses itself to the continuing problem of political and economic integration of the minorities into the Great Chinese state. Article 4 states that "discrimination against and oppression of any nationality are prohibited". Article 144 stipulates that the head of each autonomous area be chosen from the nationality residing there. While Article 121 mandates the use of the local languages in everyday government functions.[43]

There is no doubt that the policies initiated in the 1980s have given the minorities more room for articulating practices and policies specific to their own cultural traditions. Major adjustments have been made to development policies. With the socialist modernization drive, reform of the economic structure, 'opening to the world' and activisation of the economy form part of development policy in minority areas also.[44] The government has taken special measures such as reduction or exemption of various taxes in minority areas. The new economic policies have created new opportunities for entrepreneurial minority people. Efforts are being made to fully explore the strength of the minorities, advantages of various minority areas mainly in such spheres as supply of natural resources, special skills of the local people etc. However, recent trends have also had the adverse effect of increased pressure on the minority areas. They have become 'boom areas' for entrepreneurial Hans who flood into these areas, creating condition reminiscent of the 'The Wild West'.[45]

Deng's revolution has not introduced any basic change in China's minority nationalities policy,[46] except that it made more earnest effort to implement the various provisions of regional autonomy as enshrined in the Constitution. The various provisions marked quantitative changes which not only sought to ideologize but Hanize the minority nationalities.[47]

The protection of minority languages, guaranteed in the constitution, is yet to be implemented in most of the minority areas. Similarly, the notion of 'regional autonomy' needs proper interpretation in the interests of minorities nationalities.

To sum up, the whole of Chinese policy from 1949 right down to the present day has been aimed at unification that is assimilation. In general, shifts in minority policies have followed shifts in the Chinese Communist Party's orientation, with radical, leftist period such as the Great Leap Forward (1958 - 59) and the Cultural Revolution (1966-76) marked by efforts to eradicate ethnic differences and impose Han standards and practices on the minorty peoples. China began to reverse these policies after 1978. More rights were granted to minorities to protect their cultures. The experiences of Chinese minorities illustrate that various attractive policies failed to produce the same effect in practice and the 'National Question' still demands better solution.

Composition and Distribution of Ethnic Groups in Former Soviet Central Asia/Soviet Union

The former Soviet Union was one of the world's largest

multi-ethnic countries with its vast territory. It has a one of the most diverse and heterogeneous populations in the world; according to Soviet ethnic specialists there are 120 peoples and 140 distinct ethnic identities. Among them 22 major ethnic groups are made up of more than one million people each. They are Russians, Ukrainians, Belorussians, Uzbeks, Tatars, Kazakhs, Azerbaydzhanis, Armenians, Georgians, Lithuanians, Jews, Moldavians, Germans Chuvases, Latvians, Tadzhiks, Poles, Mordvinians, Turkmen, Bashkirs, Estonians, Kirghiz. Russians are by far the largest nationality (145.07 million, 1989 census), and the Ukrainians still greatly exceed the rapidly growing Muslim Central Asian nationalities.[48] The population of Central Asian region consists of three main elements - Turkic (Uzbeks, Kazakhs, Karakalpaks Kirghiz and Turkmen), Slavs (Russians, Ukrainians and Belorussians), and Iranians (Tadjiks). According to 1989 census. Russians constitute 50.6 per cent of the Total Soviet population and the Central Asian peoples formed only 12 per cent (approximately. of the total population.

The distribution of various ethnic groups is influenced by their lifestyles. Russians dominated the urbanized ares in various republics of the Central Asian Region. Most of the minority groups continued to remain on steppes, mountainous regions and agricultural lands. Their deep attachment homeland, native language, life-styles, general conservatism, low skills in Russian language acted as deterrent to migration.

The non-Russian republic nations view their traditional homelands as their very own territory within they have the right to cultural and communal, and political dominance. This is in contrast to the perception of the Russian population which perceives the border lands as an extension of Russia and themselves as political and economic benefactors and Kulturtrager[49] (representatives of culture).

Under Tsarist and Soviet rule the people of this region had

traumatic experiences. It had been a dumping ground for various nationalities. The socio-economic transformation of this region, over the years, led to the emergence of a qualitatively new and complex situation. In some Central Asian republics Russians and other ethnic minorities form the core of the population. For example, in Kazakhstan, Russians constitute 41 per cent and Kazakhs only 36 per cent.[50]

A brief note of Nationalities Policy before the 1917 Revolution

The roots of ethnic conflict in Soviet Central Asia lie in the colonial policies of the old Russian empire during the 20th century. Tsarist nationality policy towards majority of non-Russians emphasized stubborn Russification, suppression and the divide-and-rule strategy of deliberately provoking national, racial, and religious antagonism. The stress on Great Russian Nationalism was intended to, and in a measure did, build support for the autocracy among other nationalities, particularly in the border lands. It was only to kindle separatist aspirations and to unleash centrifugal tendencies which threatened the disintegration of the Empire.[51]

Through the succeeding Soviet era various methods were tried and applied, at different times and in different regions. In Central Asia political and social institutions and usages were suppressed and subverted. However, the common history of the centuries old Islamic unity made for a uniform response to nationality policy in this region.[52]

The revolution in 1917 brought to the fore not only class spirit, but also the national self-awareness of the formerly oppressed and discriminated peoples, which manifested itself, in particular, in their attempts to acquire national statehood. The central problem in Soviet Nationality Policy has been to maintain a delicate balance between two conflicting interests; to assure the continued dominance of the Russian majority and of its values, language and cultural heritage, and at the sametime to reduce the alienation of non-Russian nationalities, and to guarantee that they will be equal, valued and respected members of Soviet multi national community. In practice, Soviet policy fluctuated between these impulses.[53]

Lenin's Nationality Policy

Lenin formulated his policy on the basis of Marxist notions. At the same time he was aware of political potential of the minority nationalism. National-self-determination formed the core of his approach towards minority nationalities.

It offered the no-Russian subjects the theoretical right to independent statehood. His generosity was due to his strong belief that the minorities could not separate themselves even if they wanted to do so, because of the prevailing poor socio-economic conditions. By offering them more than what they wanted on a take-it-or-leave-it basis, he denied them realistic alternatives that lay somewhere between assimilation and separatism. Lenin believed all along, that the right to self-determination should be employed to end demands for national independence, and not to satisfy them.[54]

Lenin changed his attitude towards minorities in the interest of Russia's stability in later years. During 1918-20 Lenin devoted his attention to the establishment of institutional and administrative apparatus that would become the framework of a powerful and centralized Soviet State—the State Narkomnets[55] (The Peoples Commissariat for Nationality Affairs) and the Communist Party. A number of republics were formed on ethnic lines and appropriate degree of internal autonomy was granted. The expression 'national in form but socialist in content', aptly described the reconciliation effected by the Bolsheviks in their nationality policy between the rival claims of nationalism and socialism.[56]

In 1921 Lenin introduced New Economic Policy (NEP) which was aimed at placating the peasantry and consolidating Soviet rule. As the non-Russian nations were largely composed of peasants, the inauguration of NEP inevitably had implications for Soviet Nationalities policy. Symbols of nationhood to a number of national groups were granted. National languages and cultures were developed. Nations assumed political responsibilities and this was done through the promotion of native cadres. Lenin believed that this process could expedite the rise of the 'new socialist man' who would be capable of ridding himself of national prejudices,[57] with its persisting thrust on radical and internationalist ideology. This was the goal to which Lenin remained faithful until the very end.

Lenin's policy was, however, entirely inadequate as a solution to the complex national problem. By offering the minorities virtually no choice between assimilation and complete independence, it ignored the fact that they desired neither. He looked upon nationalist sentiments as a force suitable for exploitation in the struggle for power. However, in Lenin's view, the slogan of self-determination was to prove as a successful psychological weapon towards winning the support of the national movements which had developed, in all their magnitude during the revolutionary period.[58]

Every Soviet leader from Stalin to Gorbachev, sought to derive legitimacy for his party and government from Lenin's interpretation. The same holds true for the legitimization of the nationalities policy which is usually described as the Leninist nationalities policy.

During 1920s Korenzatsiia (nativization) was in practice. This programme advocated the equality of the non-Russian languages and cultures vis-a-vis the Russian languages and culture. This policy sought to legitimize an urban-based revolution in a predominantly agricultural multi-ethnic state by encouraging the development of distinct national cultures.[59] Many books were published in native languages. Korenzatsiia set the stage for Soviet Union's current crisis for authority among non-Russians. In the process of legitimization, it created the social bases necessary for multi-culturalism.

By the end of 1920s Stalin began to abandon NEP and launched his scheme which was somewhat different from that of Lenin.

Stalin's Nationality Policy

Stalin was dedicated to re-establishing the complete authority of the central government by making the Russian republic the core of the federation. According to him: A nation is a historically constituted, stable community of people, formed on the basis of a common language, territory, economic life, and psychological make-up manifested in a common culture.[60] History, language, territory, economy and a common culture were the five 'Stalinist categories' that acted as criteria in the 1920s and 1930s to designate, and in some cases to form, national entities. But Stalin, an advocate of diversification, did not extend such freedom to the party.[61]

Stalin launched Collectivization, the rural terror which was completed by 1937. Under this campaign, Kazakhstan suffered the worst. During 1930s most of the USSR's political and cultural elite was exterminated. Between 1941-1945 a number of nationalities were deported en masse to Soviet Asia at horrific cost in lives and suffering. His repressive measures included destruction of local economic autonomy that had existed under NEP, imposition of Cyrillic alphabet, arbitrary redrawing of boundaries, rewriting of histories to emphazie the progressive character of the Russian imperialism and end of criticism of Great Russian Chauvinism. All these were to be giant steps in Stalin's subordination of ethnic minorities. These dictatorial measures far from obliterating national identities and loyalties, served to strengthen them. Modern urban elites and cultural intelligentsia provided critical leadership in the process of national revival in subsequent decades.[62]

Thus, one of the ironies of Soviet Nationality Policy in operation was that though it seemed to place great emphasis on the subordination and suppression of minority peoples and cultures and even their ultimate 'Sliyanie' (merging) into the Russian people and culture, some of the Stalin's key policies tended to have just the opposite effect. The basis on which USSR was organised—despite denial of national autonomy—preserved and even strengthened minority identification. The concept "national in form socialist in content" was while designed to curtail nationalist aspirations, it (national in form) actually served to keep ethnic traditions alive.[63]

Nationality Policy after Stalin

Stalin's immediate successor N.S Khrushchev, started the process of de-Stalinisation in 1953, while Brezhnev's policies sought to make further reform. Pressure on Russians as well as non-Russians was considerably minimised. Their polices brought much greater freedoms of expression, the rehabilitation of parts of national cultures and a less twisted interpretation of history than those that existed under Stalin. Indigenisation of cadres resumed, though a solid convention was established that certain key officials in the republics, the most important being the Party Second Secretaries, should generally be Russian watchdogs over the activities of the native administrations.[64]

Khrushchev envisioned his political future on a highly ambitious scheme that was to have grave consequence for the Kazakh nation. "The treatment of the Kazakhs was to demonstrate that the post Stalin leadership was quite prepared to ride a roughshod over a non-Russian nation in the name of economic exigencies." The Kazakhs, who were already decimated by Stalin's brutal Collectivization drive. underwent a second major trail within a quarter of a century in the form of innocuously sounding "Virgin Lands Scheme".[65]

Just before the implementation of the scheme, Kazakh party was purged. Party leadership was replaced by Slavs. Launched in February 1954, the programme was aimed at transforming the vast areas of untilled steppe in Kazakhstan and South-western Siberia into new grain producing regions. Hundreds of Thousands of 'volunteers' were sent from the European parts of the USSR to settle and cultivate the supposedly idle areas of Kazakhstan, where the Kazakhs had for centuries bred livestock. For the Kazakhs the scheme represented a colonization that threatened their very survival and by 1959, their share in the population of their own republic had dropped to under a third.[66] The resistance of the Kazakhs was overridden.

After the Twentieth Party Congress, Khrushchev's nationality policy took a new course. He condemned some of Stalin's crimes and admitted that under Stalin there had been 'monstrous' and 'gross' violations of the basic Leninist principles of the nationalities policy of the Soviet state, namely the entire nations had been deported on spurious grounds.[67]

Khrushchev's de-Stalinisation programme revived national cultures and led to the growth of national assertiveness. By 1958 more liberal course in nationalities policy began to backtrack probably in order to reduce national distinctions. An aggressive policy against the vestiges of capitalism, among which he included nationalism, religion and improper attitude towards socially useful labour, was started.[68] As a result, there was a shift of emphasis in nationality policy away from promotion of the 'flourishing' of the cultures of the peoples of the USSR, to the acceleration of their eventual 'fusions' or 'merger'. Many purges in non-Russian republics went on. The Twentysecond Party Congress crystallized Khrushchev leadership's assimilationist policy. Anti-religious, and anti-national measures were on the rise during the last three years of Khrushchev era.

Brezhnev's Nationality Policy

After a few months of Khrushchev's removal in 1964 Brezhnev came into power. He was more tactful in his references to nationality policy than Khrushchev. As far as Central Asia is concerned it was a period of remarkable political stability. The tenures of the republican first secretaries were marked by unprecedented longevity.[69] Initially he ignored various social and national tensions that had made themselves pronounced. But the result of 1970 census came as a shock and forced the Soviet leaders to go back to seriousness in dealing with nationality problem. The factors that contributed to this outcome are stagnation of the Russians, demographic explosion of non-Russians especially the Muslim population, low-levels of migration and decline in the use of Russian.

Brezhnev's overall strategy had important impact on his treatment of the non-Russian elites. They were given enough freedom to run their republics so long as nationalism was kept under control and the economic performance was not too disastrous. As a result bureaucrats often ruled in lethargic, corrupt, and nepotistic style, and these very features of the Stalin's economic policy thrived the most in Central Asia.[70] His period was later discredited and euphemistically labelled as the 'period of stagnation.' Brezhnev was prompted to speak out in favour of more cautious policy on nationalities at the 26th Party Congress. This approach was continued by Andropov and Chernenko, who were familiar with nationality problems.[71]

Gorbachev's Nationality Policy

Gorbachev rose to power in March 1985. The epoch of democratisation in April 1985 placed Soviet multiethnic state in a complex and historical situation. Gorbachev faced a formidable accumulation of problems, economic stagnation, inefficiency, corruption, mismanagement and above all unexpected rise in ethnic tensions. He launched Perestroika and Glasnost with a view to solve the crisis in Soviet Union at various levels.

His initial pre-occupation with economic and political reform and focus on efficiency undermined the importance of ethnic relations. Gorbachev is a Russian, whose whole career has been passed within the Russian Republic and this may help to explain a certain insensitivity to the minorities problems as evident in the early period of his rule. Since 1985, in his nationalities policy he largely reacted to events rather than shaped them.[72]

Gorbachev did not formulate any specific policy to deal with the nationalities. His liberalizing policies to political and economic sphere had ethnic consequences. Central Asia remained a major problem. In Central Asia he carried out massive purges of political leaders under the guise of exchange of cadres and fighting corruption. In Kazakhstan, the replacement of Kunayev, the First Secretary of Communist Party of Kazakhstan by an ethnic Russian, Kolbin, led to violent demonstrations. Similar events occurred in the neighbouring republics. Baltic and Caucasus regions also witnessed ethnic conflicts. After Kazakh riots the issue of ethnic relations became the centre of attention of Soviet authorities. Gorbachev realized that the nationalities question was not a peripheral one but stood at the heart of the issue of reform itself.

Rise of ethnic nationalism has become a major component of Soviet domestic politics since late 1980s and early 1990s. Soviet Nationality Policy has had the effect of heightening the awareness of the dominant republican nationalities and their national identities. Since 1989 many Union republican nationalities and their national identities. Since 1989 many Union republics adopted legislation making the vernacular language of the republic the 'official language' for the conducting of government business within the republic.[73]

Democratization, glasnost and pluralism have had significant impact on the various national groups in Gorbachev's era. While democratization has encouraged people to participate, glasnost has allowed them to articulate their feelings, and pluralism has legitimized the rights of groups to form on the basis of a consciousness of self-interest. The idea of Khozraschet (economic self-balancing) has been applied to republican units as a basis for greater economic and political independence.[74].

The leaders of the communist party of the Soviet Union addressed the problems of nationalities in the USSR at a plenum of the Central Committee in September 1989. They condemned 'over centralization' that has happened in the past. Complete political rehabilitation of peoples who were subjected to repressions and mass deportation was called for. Tendencies for secession by the union republics, and formation of independent Communist parties were ruled out. A second chamber of the legislature of union republics with representatives of national groups living in the area was suggested. Earnest efforts were made to contain the centrifugal republican forces by a mixture of policies that gave recognition to linguistic and political aspirations of the non-Russian nationalities. None of them could stop the eventual break-up of the Soviet Union in 1991.

Today most Soviet and Western scholars admit that, contrary to the Marxist-Leninist postulates, ethnic consciousness does not necessarily decline as society moves towards modernization or socialism. The conflicts in communist and post-communist worlds clearly demonstrate the rise of ethnic consciousness.

Comparison of Chinese and Soviet Nationalities Policies

China and the former Soviet Union derived their policies

toward nationalities from the tenets of Marxism-Leninism. Both attempted to solve national question in an appropriately socialist manner. While only eight per cent of China's population are non-ethnic Chinese (non-Han) half of the USSR's are non-Russian. The motivating force behind the minority policies in most of the multi-national states is to achieve integration and assimilation with the majority group. When People's Republic of China was formed in 1949 broad agreement existed on adopting Soviet model for a wide variety of policy areas in China. The Chinese Communists looked to Marxist ideology and Soviet practice for lesson to be drawn to formulate their own policy on the management of their minority problems.[75] By then the USSR already had had three decades of experience in dealing with national question.

During Bolshevik revolution, to contain nationalist movements, self-determination and secession were granted to the oppressed nationalities under Tsarist rule. After 1917, their offer was taken literally by several minority groups and "...a number of nationalities seceded from Russia".[76] leading Lenin to reappraise his position on federation. Stalin made it clear that self-determination "ought to be understood not as the right of self-determination of the bourgeoisie but of the toiling masses of a given nation. The principle of self-determination ought to be used as a means in the struggle for socialism and to be subordinated to the principles of socialism."[77]

Chinese Communist Party also promised the minorities the right of self-determination and autonomy prior to the revolution. The manifesto of the party's second Congress in 1922 proclaimed Mongolia, Tibet and Turkistan to be autonomous states and envisioned their voluntary unification with China proper in a Chinese Federated Republic.[78] In 1931 a resolution of First-All-China Congress of Soviets clearly stated "national minorities shall have the right to determine for themselves whether they wish to leave the Chinese republic and create their own independent state,or whether they wish to join the Union of Soviet republics, or form an autonomous area inside the Chinese Soviet Republic."[79]

In post 1931 period CCP replaced 'self-determination' with a vague concept of 'national regional autonomy'. Mao propounded this new line in 1934, it was felt that the solution to national question was not independence nor autonomy but "free union of all nationalities". This notion is well received by Mao's successors till date.

Unlike the Soviet Union, which was a federation, the PRC followed unitary and politically centralized system. A federal system can better deal with regional (local) interests than a unitary one in theory. But Soviet Union and China both could not find a reasonable solution to minority problems. The policies of liberalization/democratization in both the multi-national countries resulted in unprecedented events.

Perestroika and glasnost of Gorbachev in the Soviet Union heralded a series of ethnic conflicts and the first major disturbance occurred in Alma-Ata (now Almaty) the capital of Kazakhstan in December 1986. In China,Deng's four modernization processes began in late 1978. But incidentally during the same period as in Soviet Union anti-Chinese demonstrations were held in Lhasa, in September, 1987. The anti-government feelings in both the cases seemed to be the result of oppressive policies carried out by the Communist regimes in minority areas—suppression of language, culture, religion of the nationalities, destruction of mosques, temples, banning minority institution etc.

The nationalities policies aimed at assimilation and integration in both the states. Instead, over the years domination (Russification and Sinification) made its presence felt. Great

Russian Chauvinism, and Great Han Chauvinism perpetuated nationalist aspirations among minority ethnic groups. Demands for 'real autonomy', 'true self-determination' have been expressed in the form of slogans at various demonstrations especially since mid-1980s.It is now accepted by Soviet and Chinese analysts that certain policies of the past in these countries were mistaken, failed and should not have been attempted, and that, infact they (for example Stalin's repressions, Mao's campaigns) led to human and economic disasters.

When the Soviet Communist Party collapsed in 1991, there was a background of economic crisis, ethnic upheaval, and the emergence of elected alternatives to its leaders.But in China as early as 1989, inflation, corruption and simmering unrest in Tibet did not add up to a comparable threat. The regime could be sustained only with military force. As communism collapsed in Eastern Europe and the Soviet Union during the following years, Deng and his fellow geronotocrats congratulated themselves on having used the PLA to preserve the power it had won for them 40 years before. But they still faced the problem of transforming a short term expedient into a long term solution.[80]

In the wake of the demise of the Soviet Union,non-Chinese are increasingly aware that under inter-national law they may have a right to self-determination and they are beginning to think the unthinkable.[81] But there is no Gorbachev and certainly no Yeltsin on the horizon. And people also realize that independence might bring more problems than it may solve when they lock at the Commonwealth of Independent States struggling to catch up with the on going globalization/liberalization of economies and at the same time coping with domestic problems. Instead the non-Chinese nationalities seem to prefer 'autonomy' in true sense of the term.

The degree of democratization in Soviet Union was greater than in China and the military played insignificant role in containing ethnic uprisings. Therefore, the consequences of ethnic disturbances, in both the cases, were different. These outcomes and selected aspects will form the contents of Chapter VI.

Foot Notes:

1. George Mosley, *The Party and the National Question in China,* (Cambridge, MIT Press, 1966) p. 29.
2. Donald R. DeGlopper, 'Chinese Nationality Policy and the Tibetan Question', *Problems of Communism,* Nov-Dec. 1990, p. 82.
3. Ibid.
4. Liu Xingwu and Alatan, "China's policy towards Her Minority Nationalities", *Social Scientist* vol. 16 No.1 Jan 1988 (N. Delhi) p.116.
5. Tom A. Grunfeld, 'In Search of Equality: Relations between China's Ethnic Minorities and the Majority Han' *Bulletin of Concerned Asian Scholar,* Vo.17, No.1 Jan-March, 1985, p.55.
6. Harold Bockman, 'The Brewing Ethnic Conflict in China and their Historical Background', in Kumar Rupesinghe, et. al. (ed.) *Ethnicity and Conflict in a Post—Communist World,* (New York St. Martin Press, 1992), p. 186.
7. Conrad Brandt, Benjamin Schwartz & *John K. Fairbank, A Documentary History of Chinese Communism,* (London, Press, Allen and Unwin, 1952), p.64.
8. See George Mosley,op. cit., n.1, p.49.
9. Brandt, et. al., op. cit, n.7 p.223.
10. Dawa Norbu, "Chinese Communist Views on National Self-determination : Origins of China's National Minorities Policy", *International Studies,* (New Delhi), vol.24, no.4, 1988.
11. Ibid pp. 327-28.
12. Donald R.DeGlopper, op. cit,n.2,p.82.
13. Su Kequin,"continue to Train Minority National Cadres" Minzu Tuanjie (Nationalities Solidarity), *Mztj,* 1961, p. 5.
14. James C.F.Wang, *Contemporary Chinese Polictics,* (New Jersey, Prentice Hall, Inc, 1980), p. 141.
15. Quoted by June Teufel Dreyer 'The People Republic of China: in Robert G. Wirsinged. *Protection of Ethnic Minorities: Comparative Perspectives,* (New York, Pergamon Press, 1981) p. 150.
16. Ibid ., p. 151.
17. Ismail Amat reports in *China Today,* vol. XLI, no.7 p. 13.
18. Harald Bockman, op.cit, n.6, p.189.

19. Donald McMillen. *Chinese Communist Power and Policy in Xinjiang (1949-1977)*, (Boulder Co. Westview Press, 1979), p.86.
20. Mao-Tse-tung 'Criticize Great Hanism' (March 16,1953) in *Selected Works of Mao-Tse-tung*, vol. V. (Peking Foreign language Press, 1977), p. 87-88.
21. Dreyer, op. cit, n. 15, p. 154.
22. George Mosley, *Consolidation of South China Frontier,* (Berkeley, University of Califoirnia Press, 1973), p.119.
23. Dreyer, op,cit,n.15.pp.154-155.
24. Dreyer, *China's Forty Millions* (Cambridge, Harvard University Press 1976) pp. 182-189.
25. George Mosley, "China's Fresh Approach to the National Minority Question", *China Quarterly*, (London), n.24, Oct-Dec, 1965.
26. Dreyer op.cit., n. 24 pp. 262-263. and McMilln. op. cit., n. 19, pp.
27. Dreyer op. cit.n.15, p. 156.
28. Ibid.
29. Christopher S. Wren, "Islam After Persecutions, Rebounds in China", *New York Times*, June 15, 1983, p.12
30. Tom Grunfeld op. cit. n.5 p.64.
31. Dereck J. Waller, *The Government and Politics of People's Republic of China* (London Hutchinson, 1981), p. 165.
32. Dreyer op. cit, n.15, p. 156.
33. Ibid. p.157
34. Dreyer.op. cit.,n.24 p.56
35. *Lhasa Radio Report*, April 20, 1971.
36. Dreyer, "China's Quest for a Socialist *Solution' Problems of Communism*, vol. 24, no.5. Sept-Oct 1975 p. 58.
37. Dreyer, op cit. n.24. p.239-240.
38. Dreyer op. cit. n.15, pp.157.
39. Ibid. p.158.
40. Text of the 1978 Constitution, *Beijing Review* Vol 21. no.11, March, 17, 1978, pp. 5-14.
41. Ye Yonghua, Marxist - Leninist View of Nationality discussed, Yunnan Rinbiao, April 3, 1981, in *Joint Publications, Research service*, June 17,1981 p.39-41.
42. "State Nationalities Affairs Commission Meeting", *Xinhua* April

15, 1982 in *Summary of World Broadcasts* part 3, The Far East, April 25, 1982.

43. 'Constitution of the People's Republic of China',*Beijing Review* 52 (Dec. 27, 1982), pp 12,27 28.
44. Liu Xingwu and Alatan, op. cit n. 4, pp.158-159.
45. Harald Bockman, op. cit, n. 6, p. 191.
46. Cf. Deng Xiaoping, "On the Minority Nationalities". *Chinese Law and Government* vol 14, no. 4 1981-82.
47. Dawa Norbu, 'China's Policy towards Minorities Nationalities' in Warikoo and Norbu ed. *Ethnicity and politics in Central Asia*, (New Delhi, South Asia Publishers, 1992). 154.
48. David Lane, *Soviet Society under Perestroika*, (London. Unwin and Hyman, 1990) pp. 162-163).
49. Rasma Karklins, *Ethnic Relations in the USSR*, (London, Allen Unwin,1986) p. 207.
50. Source: *Time* March 12, 1990.
51. Merle Fainsod, *How Russia is Governed* (Cambridge Harvard Univ. Press, 1979).
52. Tereska Rakowska Harmstone, *Russia and Nationalism in Central Asia: The case of Tadzhikistan* London 1971), p.1.
53. Gail W. Lapidius The Soviet Nationality Question' in Alexander Dallina and C. Rice ed., *The Gorbachey Era* (California, Stanford,1987) p.77.
54. Helene Carrere d' Encausse in Jermey Azrael ed. *Soviet Nationalities Policies and Practices* (New York Praeger 1978), p.40.
55. Ibid p. 41.
56. R. Vaidyanath, *The Formation of Soviet Central Asian Republics* (New Delhi 1967) p.265.
57. Helene Carrere de'Encausse, op. cit., n.54 p.47.
58. Richard Pipes, *The Formation of Soviet Union: Communism and Nationalism (1917-1923)* (Cambridge: Harvard University Press, 1954), p.49.
59. George Liber, 'Korenzatsiia, Restructuring Soviet Nationality Policy in the 1920s', *Ethnic and Racial Studies* Vol. 14 No.1 Jan, 1991.
60. Stalin Works, vol.2 (Moscow Foreign Language Publishing House, 1955), p.300.
61. Rene' Tangac, "Soviet Response to the Minority Problem" in

Gerard Chaliand ed. *Minority Peoples in the Age of Nation-States* (Delhi, Ajanta Publications, 1989), p.102.

62. G.W Lapidius, "Gorbachev's Nationalities Problem", *Foreign Affairs* (Fall 1989), pp. 92-108.
63. Dan N. Jacobs and Theresa M. Hill in Joseph L. Noges ed. *Soviet Politics* (New York, Praeger, 1985), p. 164.
64. Dominic Lieven, *Gorbachev and Nationalities* (London, Centre for Security and Conflict Studies Nov. 1988) p.5.
65. Bohdan Nahalyo and Victor Swoboda, *Soviet Disunion* (New York: Free Press, 1989) p.115.
66. Ibid, p. 116.
67. Khrushchev's *Secret Speech*, p. 58, 60-61.
68. Bohdan Nahalyo & Victor Swoboda, op. cit, n.65, pp. 121-124.
69. Martha Brill Olcott 'Central Asia: The Reformers Challenge a Traditional Society' in Lubomyr Hajda and Mark Beissinger ed. *The Nationalities Factor in Soviet Politics and Society* (Bouleder Colorado, Westview, 1990), p.257.
70. Dominic Lieven, op. cit.n.64, p.6.
71. Boris Meissner, 'Implication of Leadership for Soviet Policies', in Kinya Nessieki ed., *The Soviet Union in Transition* (London, Westview, 1987) p.58.
72. Dominic Lieven op.cit. n.64, p.11.
73. Dominic Lieven op. cit. n. 64, p. 11.
74. Ibid.p.187
75. Yeshi Choedan in Warikoo and Norbu ed, op.cit.n.47, pp.187-188.
76. See D.Kaushik, *Central Asia in Modern Times*. (Moscow: Progress Publishers, 1970), p.132.
77. Issac Deutscher, *Stalin; A political Biography* (New York: Oxford University press, 1981), pp. 184-185.
78. Mosley, op. cit, n.1, p.48.
79. Ibid, p. 164.
80. Roderick MacFarquhar *The politics of China* (1949-1989) (New York, Cambridge 1993), p.4.
81. James D. Seymour, 'Toward and East Asian Federation of Independent states' *Bulletin of Concerned Asian Scholars*. (Boulder:Colorado), Vol. 24, n. July-September, 1993, p. 94.

3

Comunist Economic Reforms (1980-1990) and the Emergence of Civil Societies

Communist reforms have been a major policy thrust towards minority areas in Communist states with different ethnic groups. The main objective of these reforms is to assimilate and integrate the minority nationalities into a 'majority whole'. Besides they want the world to believe that these nationalisties and their respective home lands are in a better position in terms of material progress than others. This chapter analyses that nature and content of reforms launched since communist takeover of Tibet and Kazakhstan. Focus will be on the reforms in the last decade—Deng's modernization policies and Gorbachev's perestroika and glasnost. Towards the end, the impact of these reforms on ethnic relations in both the cases will be discussed.

Reforms in Tibet (1950-1980) An Overview

At the time of incorporation of Tibet into Communist China, it was a primitive land with a feudal social structure and a preindustrial economy. For the newly emerged Communist China,

Soviet path to socialism was thought to be the most modern to follow Soviet economy emphasized the development of heavy industry and the rapid collectivisation of agriculture. In Chinese terms, this meant extending party as well as People's Liberation Army (PLA) control over all regions and provinces and reorganising a unified bureaucracy starting afresh to build up heavy industry and carrying out basic land reforms throughout the country.[1] The Han referred to Tibet as a land of 'three great lakhs', (fuel, communication, people) and of 'three abundances' (poverty, oppression, terror of the super natural) The initial tasks the Chinese set to themselves were to survey the land, restructure the local governing organs and establish a network of transportation and communication facilities.[2] Hence within a decade of communist rule in Tibet, roads were contructured, communications network was introduced and books and pamphlets were published in Han and Tibetan languages. All these developments took place within a decade of Communist rule in Tibet.

Initially, there was no pressure for reform and although many cadres were sent to Tibet, they made Tibetans believe that they had come to Tibet to help the Tibetans and they would leave when Tibet is 'improved'.[3] Their actions proved they had different motives. The interference of Peking in the domestic affairs of Tibet became more pronounced year after year.Economic exploitation was accompanied by the attempt to destroy the country's religious traditions, to impose a social order founded on collectivisation.[4] Resistance to Chinese reforms began in Amdo and Khan in 1956 when democratic reforms were first announced.Later, a major rebellion took place in 1959. The PLA brought the whole of Tibet under its control. The socialits frenzy of the 'Great Leap Forward' led the Chinese to pursue reforms despite increasing revolt in various parts of Tibet. As revolt in Tibet escalated, the Chinese gradually abandoned the strategy of the nationalities policy in favour of coercion. The situation in Tibet was a result, in part, of the policies of the Great Leap, but the revolt and the measures taken to suppress it also contributed to the militarisation and xenophobia of Chinese politics at the time. The Tibetan Revolt was a major international embarrassment for the Chinese and for Mao; it must be considered one of the factors in Mao's eclipse and in the retrenchment policies of the early 60s.[5]

The Tibetan Autonomous Region was established in 1965, but Han Officials have continued to dominate the most senior echelon of the Party. III conceived agricultural innovations—such as the introduction of wheat in areas unsuitable for it—resulted in serious famine between 1961 and 1964 and again in the late 1960s, [6] which was unknown in Tibet's history. Food was taken from Tibetans for the Chinese in Tibet and for the provinces adjacent to Tibet. Thousands of Tibetans who had been imprisoned after the revolt were confined in agricultural labor camps where they produced food for the Chinese while they themselves were starved.[7]

From 1966 onwards, to a much greater degree than any Chinese province or region, Tibet suffered agony from the horrors of the cultural revolution. Monasteries were destroyed across the country. According to the Chinese government's most faithful Tibetan ally, Ngapo Ngawang Jigme, the cultural revolution dragged all of China into an abyss of suffering and pain. Tibet was caught up in a groundswell that suddenly placed all its promising achievements in jeopardy. "Taking Tibet's actual conditions into consideration", a principle advocated by China's moderates, was denounced for betraying a defeatist attitude, while the 'gradual development of Tibet' was held to signify preparing the ground for the restoration of capitalism. The 'United Front' approach based on respect for Tibet's national identity and religious beliefs, designed to win over the population to socialism, was stupidly forsaken. Religious leaders, and patriotic members of the well-to-do classes were branded monsters and demons.The monasteries seen as the vestiges of obsolete superstitions were often razed. Particularly after 1969, Communes were set up all over Tibet with no thought for productivity. These measures seriously dampened the enthusiasm of the Tibetan peasants and nomads, and production dropped, leading to a marked deterioration in the population's standard of living.[8]

Thus, during this phase of Chinese rule, all traditional social and economic institutions were destroyed-or atleast banned- and a full-scale effort was launched to transform the values and belief system of the nomads and of course everyone in Tibet and China. If there is a period where the term ethnocide could be applied, it would clearly be the decade from 1966 to 1976. It is to be noted that these years also brought increased tension between the Hans and the Tibetans.

After, the cultural Revolution, the CCP changed its emphasis from ideological struggle to economic work, initiating a restructing of the economic and social relations especially the countryside. This change of course of reform was also the result of the death of Mao in 1976. Factional strife in Tibet-during the Cultural Revolution resulted in control by the hard-line faction, associated with the former PLA cadres of the Xinjian Command, until the early 1980s. Collectivisation was continued under the guidance of Ren Rong, who emerged as the TAR party secretary. Communes which had been experimentally established in 1964, were set up in 34 per cent of the town ships of the TAR by 1970 and in 90 per cent by 1974.[10] Tibet was said to have leapfrogged the stage of co-operatives.[11] In parts of the country where resistance to communal ownership was strongest, the army was called in to help. By December 1975, the Collectivization of Tibet's countryside was virtually complete, and there were almost 2,000 communes scattered throughout almost every district of central Tibet.[12]

Another element which needs mention and which is very revealing of China's intentions in Tibet: the arrival of tens of thousands of Chinese settlers sent by the order of the central government in Peking. Their massive transfer started in earnest in 1975. A China-wide census carried out in 1982 put the number of Chinese in Tibet at 96, 000, which reflects only the number of Chinese officially registered on the government's lists, and fails to take into account their wives, children and other relatives who joined them on the roof of the world.In Lhasa, for a population of 50, 000 Tibetans, there were soon over 100, 000 Chinese. New Quarters were specially built for them, and the gray box-like buildings soon surrounded and dwarfed the old Tibetan city. According to the Tibetan government-in-exile, no less than 600, 000 Chinese were sent to Central Tibet between 1975 and 1980. This means that where as in 1912 not a single Chinese was left in Tibet after the government had expelled the last Ambans, by 1980 there was atleast one Chinese for every three Tibetan in the heartland of Tibet.[13]

In the name of liberalisation, Tibet was to become witness to another new wave of reform since 1980s on the basis of reports by fact-finding delegations.Chinese as well as Tibetan.

Modernisation and Liberalisation (1980-1990)

At its December 1978 Third Plenary session in Peking, the II Party Central Committee celebrated the victory of the party's reform-minded win led by Deng Xiaoping. During 1979-80 a much heralded programme of Liberalisation began in Tibet, following the announcement of the four modernisations' programme, which focussed on agriculture, industry, science and technology and military defence in decreasing order of importance. For the rank and file of well-disciplined party cadres, the new political credo was contained in two slogans: 'economic reform' and 'open-door policy'. The wave of reassessment of almost all former policies, as it was expressed by Hu Yaobang, General Secretary of the party, during his inspection trip to Tibet in 1980 should, to a certain extent, be regarded as a sincere effort to take a fresh look at the real political conditions.

Between 22 May and 1 June 1980, Hu Yaobang with Wan Li, the then Vice Premier toured Tibet. On May 29, Hu Yaobang made a very sincere and passionate political speech at a gathering of 5, 000 cadres in Lhasa. The slogan put forward in the speech was strive to build united, prosperous and civilised new Tibet.(Wei Jianshe Tuanjie, fuyu, wenmingde, Xin, Xizand Xiang nuli Houzheng')[14] He issued a six policy directive, First, autonomy is defined as "having the right to decide for oneself", but this definition is not extended to the political plane: it refers mainly to economic decentralization. Second, the Tibetans should be exempt from taxes and work without pay. They are also free from meeting compulsory state purchase quotas, their products may be purchased at negotiated prices. These economic concessions would last three to five years. Third, a flexible economic policy suited to the specific and actual conditions in Tibet should be carried out with a view to diversifying the whole Tibetan economy. Fourth, Beijing will further increase funds to Tibet Autonomous Region in order to develop the local economy and improve living standards. Fifth, within the socialist framework, it is necessary to make vigorous efforts to revive and develop Tibetan culture, education and science...All ideas that ignore and weaken Tibetan culture are wrong'.Lastly, the Tibetan participation in the local administration should be enlarged: full Time Tibetan cadres should account for more than two-thirds of all government functionaries in Tibet within the next two to three years. [15]

Hu's directives recognised the Uniqueness of Tibet, its

special characteristics and special needs. In principle, they sounded a positive note, for the first time since 1959 acknowledging that Tibet was infact different from China. They laid the foundation for economic and cultural development during the 1980's.[16] A series of measures for revitalization of Tibet were on.

The exemption of Tibetan farmers and herder's from taxes and quota sales was obviously popular. It had been partly offset by imposition of quotas according to which farmers and nomads must sell a proportion of their produce at fixed prices to government officials.[17] As in China, the rural economy was decollectivised, and land and animals were distributed among commune members. The replacement of collectives with a house hold (or'tent hold') respon-sibility system has opened up opportunities for private initiative, and the nomads in particular appear to have prospered.[18] They used their profits to rebuild and restaff local monasteries. Owing to the liberalization and de-collectivization of the rural sector since 1979, grain production rose to 467,000 tons in 1987, a per capita average of 233 pounds. In 1990, grain production was said to have reached 560,000 tons, 0.13 per cent of China's total production figure.[19] Providing only 253 kilos of grain per capita, it remains well below the all-China average of 335 kilos for the same year.[20]

Industrialization also gained momentum since liberalization started. New towns and factories have been built in traditionally rural areas. Scientific farming and breeding of cattle has become highly valued and welcomed. But compared to other parts of China whatever development has been achieved in Tibet is negligible. Besides the policy of urban and industrial development led to rapid growth of Chinese population. Most of them became permanent settlers in these areas. Chronic poverty and over-population in neighbouring Chinese provinces push Chinese migrants into these border areas, where they find work in mining lumbering and new industrial enterprises. The Tibetan farmers in Qinghai also complain that Chinese are being se1ttled on agricultural land used by Tibetans. Though industrial development on the same scale has not taken place in the TAR, there is no reason no doubt that it would bring the same results.[21] According to Chinese government statistics, industrial production in Tibet for the month of August 1988 was just 11 million yuan or 1/10000th of China's total industrial production. This was 130 times lower than the figure for Gansu province, one of the poorest in China.[22] In 1991, the total industrial output value came to 403 million Yuan, a rise of 5.3 times that of 1959, [23] Despite these impressive figures, the standard of living of Tibetans has not improved remarkably.

There were relaxations in religious and cultural policies. On the level of daily life many of the distinctive of Tibetan cultural identity gradually re-appeared. Tibetans frequently wore traditional clothes, men grew their hair long and wore it in braids - fashions which were banned and severely punished during the Cultural Revolution. Tibetans were no longer made to feel ashamed of their culture. Religious observances also appeared in daily life. Tibetans could set up altars in their homes and they could be seen once again praying and making offerings to deities, turning prayer wheels, and visiting holy places on pilgrimage. The customary personal rituals of Tibetan Buddhism, for which Tibetans had received harsh punishments during the Cultural Revolution, could be practiced without interference from the authorities.[24]

Many temples and monasteries were rebuilt from funds collected by local people and the government. Piligrims are again allowed to visit Jokhang 'Cathedral' in Lhasa and other centres. According to a 1987 official estimate 740 monasteries and other religious sites had been renovated since 1983, and a further 230 were still being repaired. There were then 15, 000 monks in the TAR compared with an estimated 114, 000 before 1959.[25] Though officially sanctioned, the Chinese administration has sought in a variety of ways to control this process of monastic revitalization. The monasteries represent the reappearance of a Tibetan civil society, outside state control, that had lain submerged for two decades.

On educational front the establishment of the Academy of Social Sciences of Tibet was remarkable. It was set up in July 1985. For China, the schools are a powerful weapon in the campaign to sinocize Tibet, reaching far into the most remote inhabited areas.[26] In 1987 the Chinese government adopted legislation to establish Tibetan as the main official language in the TAR. Chinese officials were instructed to study the language. However, this was not put into practice. On the other hand, Tibetans were always forced to learn Chinese, but the Chinese never made a sincere effort to learn Tibetan.

Hu's demand that Chinese cadres be withdrawn from Tibet and that the government of Tibet be placed in the hands of Tibetan cadres, met with only limited success. It not only failed to yield positive results, but it produced the exact opposite of what he sought to achieve. His decision to withdraw 85 per cent of the Chinese cadres met with violent opposition. In the first place, many of the older generation of Tibetan cadres that Hu found on his visit were as opposed to Deng's reforms as their Chinese colleagues—big Han chauvinists. Trained by the military or in cadre schools, this entrenched group made its way up through the party hierarchy during the period of collectivization in Tibet. They feared such policy will erode their power. This group of old Tibetan cadres find themselves comfotable with the Chinese and no longer identify themselves with Tibetans. They may be compared with English-educated 'Babus' in India under British rule. The over seers of two decades of repression, they command no respect from ordinary Tibetans; paradoxically they have been the principal beneficiaries of the call to Tibetanize the administration of Tibet.[27]

During the liberlisation era the number of Chinese immigrants increased even more rapidly in Tibet, primarily in response to wage increments or bonuses given to Chinese willing to go there. The salary of a cadre in Tibet is often three times higher than a comparable salary 'inside' China. To be precise, in a 1987 statement to the Tibet standing Committee of the National People's Congress, the Panchen Lama complained that 'the expense of keeping one Chinese in Tibet is equal to that of four in China. Why should Tibet spend its money to feed them?' Frankly speaking, except for the lure of easy money no Chinese would like to live in Tibet's inhospitable highlands. In the towns, a whole series of occupations has changed hands; numerous work-shops and stores owned by Tibetans have been forced to close by the unexpected competition.[28] According to the most recent report published by the Department of Information of the Dalai Lama's government in exile the transfer of Chinese to Tibet has attained alarming proportions. The real fear is that if the present Chinese policy is successful—and indications are that it will be—Tibetan will be reduced to a small and insignificant minority in their own country in the same way as Manchus (35 Chinese to one Manchu), the Turkic people (3 to 1) and the Mongolians (5 to 1) have been. The object of this policy is to forcibly "resolve" China's territorial claims over Tibet by means of a massive and irreversible population transfer.[29] The Chinese authorities justify the presence of Han people proclaiming they are there to help Tibetans develop their economy and culture.

One more important reform was at the party level. The head of the regional Party in Tibet has always been Chinese, but this trend was changed. Ren Rong, whose career as a political commissar with the Tibet military region goes back to 1965, was head of the regional party from 1971 to 1980, until he was replaced on Hu's orders. His replacement was, another long-time PLA political commissar in Tibet, Yin Fatang, whose career was interrupted by the cultural revolution. Yin claimed to protect the interests of the entrenched old guard in Tibet both Tibetan and Chinese.[30] He made an important speech at the second enlarged plenary session of third Regional Chinese Communist Party Committee on 25th April 1984. He said 'in order to continue to push the work in Tibet vigorously forward and thus enable our people to become rich as soon as possible, we should first pay great attention to the following four words: change, flexibility, enliven and reform.[31] He also announced tax exemption policies (started since 1980) would be extended through, 1990, besides other concessions to peasants and herdsman to carry out commercial and other undertakings inside and outside Tibet. In 1985 Beijing replaced him with an outsider and a reformer, Wu Jinghua. Wu was committed to implementing the policy of 'openness and reform in Tibet and supported programmes to restore' Tibetan culture, religion and language.

Since 1950, with only extremely rare exception, none besides a handful of Soviet advisers and harmless 'friends of China' had been allowed to travel to China's Tibet. In 1981, Lhasa was declared an open area accessible to tourists.Since then, Tibet opened to foreign tourism (and built about half-a-dozen new luxury hotels, including a Holiday Inn in Lhasa), solicited foreign aid and development funds, and actively courted the economic participation of the exile community. The number of tourists grew rapidly—15, 000 in 1985 and 30, 000 in 1986.[32] In 1987 China earned 130 million Yaun from the 43, 000 tourists. In order to feed the exotic fantasies of the 'foreign friends', greater efforts were made to promote the restoration of some monasteries and temples.[33] As a part of this policy 200 monasteries and 700 sutra reciting halls were rebuilt and Monlam a traditional Tibetan religious festival was allowed to be celebrated with the Panchen Lama in attendance.[34] In opening up, Tibet's tourism industry has gradually flourished. At present, Tibet has 11 travel agencies and 19 tourist hotels and guest houses with 3,600 beds for foreign guests. The autonomous region has opened over 60 scenic spots to the public. Between 1980 and 1991. Tibet received 150,900 overseas tourists.[35] However, a major anti-Chinese explosion in September 1987 led the authorities to impose strict controls on foreign visitors. This rebellion was thought to be the most remarkable after the 1959 incident. (These issues will be discussed later in Chapter V)

A new development plan for TAR was announced in 1990. It called for four new economic zones, each with special role to play: a central comprehensive zone based on Lhasa, and Xigaze; an eastern zone for minerals, light industry and forestry, based on Nyingchi and Qamdo, a western border-trade centered on Ngari, and a northern animal husbandry zone centered on Naggu. Ma Lishen, the 52 year old standing deputy chairman of the autonomous region was made incharge of the plan.[36] More recently China announced the creation of a "special economic and technological zone" with incentives and preferential tax policies to attract domestic and foreign investment. The whole idea is to regularize private domestic Chinese business enterprises in Tibet and to give 'Compensatory transfer of land use right" to non-Tibetans.[37] For the first time Tibetan agricultural land was purchased by Chinese farmers in the Lhasa Valley.[38] The significance of this development for the strategy of economic reform in Tibet was made clear in a speech by Chen Kuiyuan (deputy Secretary of the Party) on 25 July 1992. He declared: "ideological obstacles to reform and opening up come mainly from the left and the old"...and economic revolution in

Tibet must be 'accompanied by a social revolution".[39] Here social revolution referred to persistence of traditional attitudes and modes of production as well as resistance of Tibetans to incorporation into a market economy. This new phase of reform once again provoked a sense of crisis in the thinking of Tibetan Cadres.[40] Tibetan struggle for real autonomy continues till date.

Reforms in Kazakhstan since Communist Takeover (1917-1985): A Review

Kazakhstan too underwent similar process of reforms, like Tibet. Here, the reform policy was designed to deal with central Asian Muslim population as a whole of which Kazakhs were a part.

After the 1917 revolution a series of declarations were addressed to the oppressed nation. A special appeal was issued specifically to the Muslims signed by Lenin in order to bring them under the 'Red Umbrella'. The central problem in the reform policy had been to maintain a delicate balance between two conflicting interests: to assure the continued dominance of Russian majority and of its values, language, and cultural heritage and at the same time to reduce the alienation of non-Russian nationalities, and to guarantee that they will be equal, valued, and respected members of a Soviet multi-national community.[41.]

Lenin formulated has policy on the basis of Marxist options, besides developing his own idiosyncratic theory of national self-determination. Statehood was given to some national groups for the first time. But artificial boundaries created confusion when Kazakh areas fell under Uzbek republic. Kazakhs were the first to experience Russian colonization. During the civil War (1918-20) Kazakhstan suffered material as well as human losses. By 1920 tens of thousands of Kazakhs had been killed and some 800,000 Kazakh-kyrgyz nomads had fled to China.

The poorer Russian settlers had also suffered horrendously in the civil war.[42] The newly formed communist Party of Kazakhstan (CPKZ) was to remain dominated by Russians, for several decades.[43] Alash Orda was the one and only nationalist party existing at that time.

In 1921 Lenin introduced New economic policy which was aimed at placating the peasantry and consolidating Soviet rule. He tried to woo the Muslim populations besides other non-Russian masses through the medium of their native languages and cultures. More than developing the economy this policy granted symbols of nationhood. Native cadres were given political responsibilities. Lenin believed that this process could speed the rise of the new socialist man who would be capable ridding himself of national prejudices[44] with its persisting thrust on radical and internationalist ideology.

During 1920's the programme of Korenzatsiia led to creation of schools of Marxist Literature in native languages. Very significant advance in culture were illustrated with the steep rise of publishing in non-Russian languages. In 1928 six book titles per 100, 000 persons were published in Kazakh language, which was less than the titles published in Uzbek and Turkomen languages teen each.[45]

By the end of 1920s Stalin began to abandon New Economic Policy and launched collectivization, the rural terror which was completed by 1937. He also replaced the old party elites by new ones. Alash members who were putting up stiff political resistance were severely attacked. In 1925 Ahmed Baytursun was the first to be purged from CPKZ.and in April 1928 several other leaders were accused of being ultra-nationalists and executed. Kazakhs were charged with having links with China along with Kyrgyz. The purges also included intelligentsia—writers, poets, doctors, scientists, engineers and others. People who had just struggled up the communist ladder by educating themselves were brought down, humiliated and executed. Of 700 writers, many of them from Central Asia, who met at the First Congress of the union of Soviet Writers in 1934, only 50 survived to see the Second Congress in 1954.[46]

Large parts of Kazakhstan, like Siberia, were turned into gulags. In 1937 in the vast Karlag Complex of labour camps around Karaganda there was a revolt by inmates which was forcibly put down after 440 prisoners were shot dead. Thousands of communists and nationalists disappeared without trace in the 1930s from these gulags.[47]

Under collectivization Campaign local economic autonomy granted under New Economic Policy was curtailed. Kazakhstan was one of the worst-affected regions during this campaign in the early 1930s to collectivize agriculture and settle nomadic peoples. According to B.Nahalya and V. Swoboda in the 1930s Kazakhstan lost through migrations, death, murder, prison, starvation and other causes 1.5 million people or one-third of the entire indigenous population. Thousands of Kazakh nomads fled to China, while many Kazakh clans took up arms, only to be crushed by Red Army cavalry units. Livestock losses were enormous as people killed their animals rather than see them appropriated by the state. The number of cattle shrank from 7.4 million head in 1929, to 1.6 million in 1933, and of sheep from 21.9 million head to 1.7 million.[48]

The new-collectives that were set up after 1929 were desparately poor. The nomads who were turned into farmers overnight had neither the tools, seed, housing, nor the machinery to carry out even the basic tasks of farming. It was not surprising that out of the 400 agronomists listed on the collectivization process only four were Kazakhs. In 1929 there were only 17, 500 communists in the whole of Kazakhstan, the majority of them Russians. Collectivization was followed by the beginnings of industrialization of Central Asia. Industrial establishments were set up in major cities. They became industrial islands in a predominantly peasant culture. Not only that they were autonomous but also had no connection with the agricultural and nomadic base around them. They were governed by Russians which widened the rural-urban divide in Kazakhstan. By the spring of 1932 famine was raging across Kazakhstan, and because it helped destroy local resistance to the communists, little help was forthcoming from Moscow.[49] There was also severe repression from the 1930s onwards and Russian immigration was greatly increased. People deported from parts of the USSR (including German, Crimean Tatars and Caucasian Peoples) were often sent to Kazakhstan, causing some resentment among the local inhabitants.[50] There was some relaxation in Communist Propaganda after the War as Russian leaders mobilized the population on the basis of Patriotism against the Germans. However, more strict communist control was to follow under Khrushchev.

Stalin's immediate successor, N.S. Khrushchev, started the process of de-stalinisation in 1953. He envisioned his political future on a highly ambitious scheme that was to have grave consequences for the Kazakh nation. The Kazakh steppes were, declared virgin territory. "The treatment of the Kazakhs was to demonstrate that the post-Stalin leadership was quite prepared to ride roughshod over a non-Russian nation in the name of economic exigencies." The Kazakhs, who were already decimated by Stalin's brutal Collectivization drive, underwent a second major trial within a quarter of a century in the form of innocuously sounding 'Virgin Lands Scheme'.[51] Ignoring fears expressed by some experts that 'Kazakhstan would re turned into a dust bowl, the authorities allocated land to hundreds of thousands of 'volunteers' from Russia and the Ukraine and ordered them to farm it. For the Russians, it was a new empty frontier country like the wild west to be civilized and developed to meet grain production targets set by Moscow.[52] It was another sign of Russian colonization for the Kazakhs.

This scheme was unsuccessful due to widespread storms and wind erosion and between 1960 and 1964 4 million hectares of farm land were ruined and 12 million hectares were damaged. This was nearly half of the land brought under cultivation in the scheme. Tselinograd, 960 kilometers northwest of Alma-Ata, was the centre of the scheme and called the Virgin Lands city. Now it has reverted back to its old Kazakh name Aqmola, or white Tombs and the wheat fields have once again become infertile grass lands.[53] This and other schemes, which included the nuclear testing sites in eastern Kazakhstan, the Baikonur space center at Leninsk and the huge industrial sites in the north and east of Kazakhstan, all attracted large numbers of ethnic Russians to the republic: the ethnic Russians proportion of the population rose from 19.7% in 1924 to 42.7% in 1959.[54] This explains the large numbers of Russians' presence even today.

Religious practice were also under attack. Anti-Islam propaganda intensified. Islamic funerals, weddings and veils were banned. The existing few Islamic schools and mosques were shut down. But after the Twentieth Party Congress, Khrushchev's policy took a new course He condemned some of Stalin's crimes and admitted that under Stalin there had been 'monstrous' and 'gross' violation of the basic Leninistic principles of the nationalities policy of the Soviet state, namely, the entire nation had been deported on spurious ground.[55]

Within the framework of central plan, the republics were asked to take initiative with regard to particular branches of economy Concessions were made to enhance the status of native languages. To some extent this period may be compared to Gorbachev's glasnost of mid 1980s. By 1958 once again liberal course began to backtrack to reduce national distinctions and to create 'Soviet man'. The policy tilted from flourishing of cultures of peoples of the USSR to the acceleration of their eventual 'fusion' or 'merger' (Sliiane). Many purges went of Secretary General of the CPKZ Zhumabai Shaiakhmetov, a Kazakh, and his deputy were replaced with two Russians, one of whom was Leonid Brezhnev. There were many revolts in gulags which were brutally suppressed. The Twenty Second Party Congress crystallyzed Khrushchev leadership's assimilationist policy. Anti-religious, and anti-national measures were on the rise during the last three years of Khrushchev.

Brezhnev came to power in 1964. This coincided with similar changes in Kazakhstan. Dinmukhamed Kunayev, a Kazakh and a Brezhnev loyalist, was promoted to the position of First Secretary of the CPKZ he became a member of politburo in 1971 and ruled Kazakhstan for twenty years, until December 1986. The results of 1970 census came as a shock and forced the Soviet leaders to deal with nationality problem more carefully than before, Brezhnev gave non Russian elites enough freedom to run their republics so long as nationalism was kept under control and the economic performance was not too disastrous. As a result lethargy, corruption, nepotism prevailed and there was slow progress in the economic sphere. In Kazakhstan, Kunayev managed to build his own power base inspite of Russian dominance in important party positions. He put members of his Dzuze clan of the Great Orda into powerful bureaucratic positions. A new Kazakh political mafia developed, owing complete allegiance to Moscow but at times pretended to take a nationalist position in order to ensure that Kazakh nationalism was not channeled into anti-Soviet feeling.[56] Brezhnev was accused of creating a period of 'stagnation'. His successors Andropov and Chernenko followed more cautious policies.

Kazakhstan also witnessed an era of stagnation under Kunayev's regime. The rampant corruption and protests by local Russians and the mafia style politics of his entourage encouraged newly elected. First Secretary of CPSU Michael Gorbachev to sack Kunayev in December 1986 and replace him by an ethnic Russian, Gennedy Kolbin. Kazakhs were very unhappy and felt insulted at this gesture, which reflected in their anti-Russian and nationalist feelings in the years ahead.

Reforms in Gorbachev Era

Gorbachev's arrival in March 1985 into Soviet Politics led to beginnings of democratization in April 1985 and placed the Soviet state in a complex and historical situation. He launched Perestraoika (Restrucring) and Glasnost (Openness) with a view to solve the Soviet crisis at various levels. Among the Central Asian Republics, Kazakhstan dominated the scene throughout Gorbachev's period with significant developments. The first and foremost event which shocked the Soviet leaders was Alma-Ata riots.Few days after Kolbin was brought to power, anti-Russian riots broke out an 17 December 1986, against his appointment. The causes consequences and nature of the riots will be discussed in detail in the next chapter (Chapter V). Martial law was imposed to control the agitating Kazakhs. In some towns it continued until the end of 1987. Gorbachev's initial occupation with economic and political reform and focus on efficiency undermined the importance of ethnic relations. His reforms unleashed an unprecedented tide of protests and demonstrations in which national grievances occupied a central place alongside economic unrest. His liberalizing policies in political and economic spheres had ethnic consequences. After Kazakh riots the issue of ethnic relations was forced to the centre of attention by Soviet authorities. Gorbachev realised that the nationalities question was not a peripheral one but stood at the heart of the issue of reform itself. Speaking at the plenary meeting of the CPSU Central Committee on January 27, 1987, Gorbachev stressed the need to present "a real picture of relations between nationalities and the prospects for their development and efforts be made to save the rising generation from the demoralising effect of (narrow) nationalism."[57]

A study group to examine public opinion in the republic was established under the auspices of Kazakhstan's Communist Party's propaganda and agitation department. Its main aim was to prevent the recurrence of such riots.[58] Many were sentenced death for provoking young people to participate in Alma-Ato riots. Resolutions were passed to improve the instruction of Kazakh as well as Russian language in schools. Besides German, Korean, Dungan languages were also to be studied as first language in several parts of the republic depending upon the pattern of local population.[59] Vigorous social policies were pursued to improve the standard of living of the people in the republic.

Meanwhile Kolbin lost the support of the CPKZ and was defeated in the election of March 1989. Nazarbayev became the First Secretary of the CPKZ. He was to emerge as the most important leader in Central Asia because of his adroit handling of the crisis that were to follow in the Soviet Union and in Kazakhstan itself.[60] Nazarbayev wanted a careful balance between the center's respect for the sovereignty of individual republics and the republics recognition of the strategic interdependence built into the Soviet state structure. He stressed the need for a 'single economic space' and a 'single strategic space', which required a centre with credible monetary and political authority. Nazarbayev was immensely popular at home amongst both his fellow Kazakhs and Russian settlers. They trusted him because Nazarbayev knew that if the Soviet state broke up, Kazakhstan's Russian population would be irrevocably antagonized and peace in the region could be jeopardized.[61]

One remarkable development in Kazakhstan, due to the policies of perestroika and glasnost was the growth of informal groups

-anti-nuclear and Green movements. The influence of these movements was so powerful that the CPKZ was forced to close Semipalatnisk for nuclear tests. One of the best known movements—Nevda—subsequently developed into People's Congress Party, the most important opposition party in Kazakhstan.

On the economic front, the reforms led to the growth of new enterprises. Contacts with foreign partners in the neighbouring East Europe and in the capitalist West grew. However, agricultural output slightly contracted due to drought situation and problems in the distribution of fertilizers. The disruption in output coupled with lax in financial policies in the USSR as a whole, helped fuel inflation. Following a long period of stable and centrally fixed prices, average retail prices rose by 84% in 1991.[62]

By 1989 with perestroika in full swing in Russia a litany of complaints arose from Central Asian leaders. Kazakhstan witnessed a series of problems—ecological imbalance, water shortage, unemployment, housing, land distribution, low productivity. Scarcity of resources etc. When the Central Asian people compared themselves to the rest of the USSR they considered themselves worse off.

Gorbachev's Perestroika and the loosening of communist control opened the floodgates of Islamic revival. The Communist Party elites in the five Muslim republics "became patrons of their national arts benefactors who helped transform state owned buildings, mosques and religious institutions and champions of the shift from Russian to their own national languages in public life.[63] Complaints about the lack of school instructions in the Kazakh language led to a decree issued in March 1987 that advocated improvents in the teaching of both Kazakh and Russian. In September 1989 the Kazakh Supreme Soviet (Parliament) adopted legislation establishing Kazakh as the official language of the republic, while Russian remained a language of interethnic communication. However, all officials communicating with the general public would be required to know both languages.[64]

Kazakh was less Islamized republic than others in Central Asia. However, Islam gave them a distinct cultural identity.[65] It was an irony that Gorbachev's policies of openness, instead of leading to political liberalization in Central Asia, greatly helped in reviving Islam and Islamic traditions. Underground groups and private prayer circles emerged into the open and began to build mosques and criticize the establishment's Muslim hierarchy. Koran was translated into native languages. In early 1990 the Qazi of Alma-Ata, Radbek Nisanbai, had himself elected Grand Mufti of Kazakhistan thus creating a separate Kazak Muslim board without consulting Moscow.[66] The immediate sign of this independent spirit in the religious revival was construction of new mosques. By October 1990, there were 90 mosques in Kazakhstan compared to 37 before.[67] A year later by October 1991, there were over 1000 new mosques in every republic of Central Asia and a new mosque was being opened every day. A year after, in 1992 thousands of mosques came into existence in each republic.[68]

In 1991 independence was thrust upon Soviet republics due to interplay of political, economic and social forces. At the time of the August coup and after Nazarbayev acted with caution. The whole of Soviet Union was under the grip of severe economic crisis. The situation was worse in the Central Asian region. But it was short-lived in Kazakhstan. There was significant improvement within a year. In October 1991 Nazarbayev signed a treaty to establish an economic community. Kazakhstan had begun the process of enacting legislation that would allow a capitalist economy, private property and foreign investment with repatriation of profits.[69] Kazakhstan was the last to declare its independence from the USSR. This tardiness was attributed to Nazarbayev's concern to preserve the delicate interethnic balance between Russians and Kazakhs in the republic and also to prevent further discussion of the cession of Kazakhstan's northern territories to the Russian Federation. Above all, it was seen as evidence of his view that the need for, and consequences of economic reform would be considerably more important than those of political change.[70] Nazarbayev has learnt this lesson from Gorbachev, who allowed political liberalization to take place before he brought about any fundamental economic changes. He gained popularity and emerged victorious in the presidential elections in December 1991.

In recent years Kazakhastan tried to lure foreign investors to develop the oil industry. Kazakhastan's relative stability and determination to privatize the economy faster than others helped her in negotiating many deals with the Western nations. The wide-ranging market reforms contained the food crisis.

Despite these appreciable developments after independence, the rural life needs more attention. Nearly three-fourths of the population still live in poor rural areas leading semi-nomadic life. In the urban areas Russians are leaving the republic fearing a Kazakh backlash. Kazakhstan also has been actively seeking the return of ethnic Kazakhs living abroad, . In 1992-93 for example, 43, 000 Kazakh arrived from Mongolia, 20, 000 from Russia and 25, 000 from Uzbekistan and other Central Asian states. Many of these newly arrived Kazakh resettlers moved into southern Kazakhstan, where they began displacing Russians, who in turn began moving to the north of the republic or into Russia.[71]

Kazakhstan witnessed a series of reforms under Soviet rule. But the processes set in motion, after Gorbachev's ascent to power, have a major role to play in deciding to country's future.

Impact of Reforms on Ethnic Relations

Two Communists giants, China and the former Soviet Union, (the former the largest and the latter the first) formulated reform policies with regard to minority nationalities, on the basis of Marxist principles. Here, the two ethnic minorities under study —Tibetans and Kazakhs—experienced similar forms of suppression under communist rule. Hence an attempt to compare them. Though they differed slightly in their terminology now and then their main objectives had been similar—to integrate and assimilate the minority nationalities into a single whole by wooing them with notions like 'self-determination' and 'Regional autonomy'

Historically speaking, Tibet had been an independent nation with veritable characteristics. It was forcibly incorporated into the Chinese state. Kazakhstan, on the other hand, had been a colony under Tsars. After the Bolshevik Revolution in 1917, inspite of persistent resistance, Kazakh territory was forcibly taken over by the Soviet leaders. Unlike Kazakhstan, Tibet was not a colony before occupation but experienced colonial hegemony since 1950 when the People's Liberation army entered this region. Mao and Lenin made an earnest attempt to bring minority national areas into socialist path by transforming economic base, social structure and ethnic composition. Tibet and Kazakhstan became victims of forced collectivization. During Collectivization period Chinese and Russians flocked to these minority regions. Industrialization followed without any concern for preconditions. Tibetans and Kazakhs suffered innumerable losses—human as well as material.

The leaders felt that by negating or suppressing native culture and languages integration would become easier. Accordingly, measures were followed to destroy symbols of national cultures. The more stronger the policies the more conscious were the ethnic minorities to their cultural heritage. Cultural

Revolution in China, and Khrushchev's anti-Islamic propaganda tried their best to test the unwavering faith of Tibetans and Kazakhs in Buddhist and Islamic principles respectively. Many temples were destroyed in Tibet. Kazakhs also lost many symbols of cultural and religious heritage.

The process that went on in China since the death of Mao is almost same as the one that took place in the USSR (and East European countries) during the ten years following the death of Stalin.[72] In China these changes took place under far more backward conditions and with a time lag of nearly twenty years. Mao and Stalin were denounced for their conservatism. The successors of Mao and Stalin initiated liberal reforms, especially Deng Xiaoping and Michael Gorbachev.

Chinese leadership proclaimed the four modernization—in agriculture, industry, science and technology and defence—in 1978. The decision on 'Economic Reform' adopted by the Central Committee Plenary meeting on October 20, 1984 was a mile stone on the way to far reaching economic and structural reforms. These reforms are aimed according to the proclamation of the leadership at establishing a new kind of socialism with Chinese characteristics (alternatively, socialism with a Chinese face) in world's largest socialist country, Seven years later, in Soviet Union, Gorbachev came to power. He launched perestroika and glasnost aimed at liberalization and democratization. These polices have had a revolutionary impact on the political socio-economic and cultural life of minority nationalities. Unprecedented events took place in Central Asian region, particularly in the largest republic of Kazakhstan.

Tibet witnessed a major rebellion in 1987 which was considered to be a great significance after 1959 disturbances. Around the same period in December 1986 first and major riot broke out after the launching of Gorbachev's reforms. These two events made the Communist leaders acknowledge the persisting nationalist aspirations which were not given due consideration under Communist rule. The reform policies aimed at assimilation and integration of the minority nationalities into a single whole proved counter-productive. Signification or Sinicization and Russification or Sovietization instead of undermining the demands for autonomy and independence strengthened nationalist feelings. In both the cases under study, religious revival took place. A new form of ethno-religious- nationalism made its presence felt in various demonstrations and disturbances in recent years. Four and a half decades of Chinese rule and seven and a half decades of Soviet rule failed to resist this powerful phenomenon. While Tibet continues its struggle for independence with greater strength than before, Kazakhstan became independent in 1991 and became a member of Commonwealth of Independent States (CIS).

Once a backward region, Tibet has achieved commendable degree of socio-economic development. Besides, with the opening of Tibet to tourists, awareness about democracy and human rights has increased. The absence of these very notions in their homeland strengthened their genuine nationalist aspirations. Similarly, in Kazakhstan, russified socio-economic progress brought dramatic change in living standards of Kazakhs. Today Kazakhstan is the most urbanized region with the largest number of Russians among Central Asian republics. In Tibet and Kazakhstan religious and cultural revival has been an unintended consequence since the onset of Communist reforms. The usage of religious symbols as forms of protest (Tibet) and as Party symbols (Kazakhstan) shows that the phenomenon is directly linked to nationalism. Tibetans and Kazakhs feel that self-determination and autonomy, promised at the time of their incorporation into communist orbits, are a mere eye-wash. Decades of Communist rule resulted in the loss of human lives and national cultures. They realize that economic reforms are a means to reduce native population to an insignificant minority. With the loosening of communist controls to pave the way for reforms since 1980s, Tibetans and Kazakhs reacted sharply to all forms of repression by the authorities. While benefiting from the communist reforms they did not ignore their ethnic origins. The conflicts, mass demonstrations, ethnic-national revival reveal the persistence of ethnic identity assertion among these two ethnic minorities.

Foot Notes:

1. Wang Chung Wu, *China and the world since 1949* (London: Macmillan, 1977), p.36.
2. Tom Grunfeld, *The Making of Modern Tibet* (Delhi, Oxford University Press, Delhi, 1987), p.117.
3. Warren Smith, 'The Nationalities Policy of the CCP and The Socialist Transformation of Tibet' in Robert Barnett and Shirin Akiner (ed) *Resistance and Reform in Tibet,* (London:Hurst & Company, 1994), p.63.
4. Carmen Leccardi, "Ethnic Conflict and Prejudice in a Colonial Context: The CAse of Tibet" *International Journal of Group Tensions,* Vol.23, no....3.1993, p.203.
5. Warren Smith in Robert Barnett and Shirin Akiner, ed., op.cit, n.3. pp.67-68.
6. John Bray, 'China and Tibet: An end to empire' *World Today* (London) vol.46, no., 12 Dec. 1990, p.221
7. Waren Smith, Op.cit, n.3, p. 68.
8. Tibetan s about Tibet, *China Reconstructs,* (Peking 1988), pp, 187-8.
9. Melvyn C.Goldstein, "Change Conflict and Continuity Among a Community of Nomadic Pastoralists" in Barnett and Akiner ed, op.cit, n, 3, p.96.
10. *Bejing Review,* July 19, 1974.
11 *Beijing Review,* July 18, 1975,
12. Pierre-Antoine Donnet, *Tibet: Survival in question* Tr. by Tica Broch (Delhi:Oxford University Press, 1994) p.85.
13. Ibid. p.86.
14. Wang Yao, 'Hu Yaobang's visit to Tibet' postscript in Barnett & Akiner ed, op cit, n.3. p.287.
15. *Foreign Broad Cast Information Service* PRC vol.1, n.108, pp.Q3-6 and Dawa Norbu 'Chinese plicy towards minority Nationalities' in K. Warikoo and Dawa Norbu ed. *Ethnicity and politics in Central Asia* (New Delhi, South Asian Publishers, 1992) .155.
16. Ronald D. Schwartz, *Circle of protest* (London, Hurst & Company, 1994), p.17.

17. John Bray, op cit, n.6, p.222.
18. Melvyn C.Goldstein and Cynthia M.Beall. "The Impact of China's Reform Policy on the Nomads of Western Tibet." *Asian Survey,* vol.6, no.6 (June 1989), p. 619.
19. *Xinhua,* 15 and 24 Feb.1991.
20. Donnet, op cit, n.12, p.148.
21. Schwartz op, cit, n.16 pp 205-206.
22. Donnet op.cit, p.148 and Xinhua 8th September 1988.
23. *Beijing Review,* vol.35, no.39, Sept.28-Oct 4, 1992, p.30.
24. Schwartz op.cit, n.16, p.16.
25. *Tibetan Review,* September 1990.
26. Donnet op.cit, n.12, p.150.
27. Schwartz op.cit. n.16, p.17 and Wanchuck Sharlo, Tseten, "China's Reforms in Tibet: Issues and Dilemmas', *Journal of Contemporary China,* vol.1, no.1, 1992, pp.34-60.
28. Donnet, op. cit., n.12, p.98.
29. *The Factors about Tibet,* Department of Information, Dharamsala, 1988.
30. Schwartz, op. cit, n. 16, p. 18.
31. *Summary of World Broad Costs,* (SWB), FE/7632/, 2 May 1984, P. BII/2.
32. Profile of Tibet (I), 'Tibet opens to the outside world' *Beijing Review,* vol.30, no.42, 19 October 1987, p.16.
33. Schwartz, op.cit, n.16, p.103.
34. Profile of Tibet (II) 'Lamaism Flourishing in Tibet' *Beijing Review* vol.30, 26 Oct.—1 Nov.1987, p.23.
35. *Beijing Review* op. cit., n.23, p.30.
36. Tibet Plans for Big Economic Growth, *China Today,* vol.40, no.10, October 1991, pp.40-41.
37. "Tibet Encourages Foreign Investment" *China's Tibet,* vol.3, no.4, Winter 1992, pp.19-20.
38. Schwartz, op.cit., n.16, p.207, n.33.
39. Lhesa Tibet Television Network in Monderin, 27, July 1992, in *FBIS* 3 August 1992.
40. Schwartz, op. cit., p.208.
41. Gail, W. Lapidus 'The Soviet Nationality Question' in Alexander Dallin & C. Rice Ed. *The Garbacher Era* (California Stanford,

1987), p. 77.

42. Ahmed Rashid, *the Resurgence of Central Asia,* (London, Zed Books, 1994), p.114.
43. Ibid.
44. Helene carere d'Encausse'Determinants aqnd Parameters of Soviet Nationality policy' in Jermey. R. Azrael ed. *Soviet Nationality policies and Practices,* (New York Praeger, 1978) p.40
45. For details, see Bohadan Nahalyo and Victor Swoboda, *Soviet Disunion,* (New York, The Free Press, 1989).
46. Ahmed Rashid, op.cit, n.42, pp.34-114.
47. Ibid.
48. Ibid, pp. 114-115.
49. Robert, Conquest *Harvest of Sorrow*, (London, Arrow Books, 1988), no.2, p.115.
50. 'Kazakhstan' Introductory Survey, *The Europa World Year Book* (London Europe Publications, 1994), p. 1675.
51. B. Nahalya and V. Swobode op.cit. no.45, p.115.
52. Ahmed Rashimd, op.cit, n.42, pp.115-116.
53. Ibid, p.116.
54. *Europa Year Book*, op.cit, n.50, p. 1675.
55. Khrushchev's *Secret Speech*, pp.60-61
56. Ahmed Rashid, op.cit, n.42, p.116.
57. John Sallnow *"Reform in Soviet-Union, Glasnost and Future,* p. 54.
58. Taras Kuzio, 'Nationalist Riots in Kazakhstan', *Cenral Asian Survey,* Vol.7, no.4, pp.79-100.
59. *SWB* Part I USSR, 8 Jan, 1989.
60. Ahmed Rashid, op.cit, n.42, p.117.
61. Ibid., p.118.
62. *Economic Review Kazakhstan* (Washington, D.C., International Monetary Fund, 1992), p.3.]
63. Marth Brill Olcott 'Central Asia's Catapult to Independence' *Foreign Affairs* (New York) Vo. 71 No.3,
64. *Europe a World Year Book* op.cit n.50 p.1675.
65. Ahmed Rashid, op.cit n.42 p.42.
66. Ahmad Rashid, 'Bless Perestroika and send Korans *Independent,* 4 June 1990.

67. 'The Islamic Challenge' *Far Eastern Economic Review,* 12 July 1990.
68. Ahmed Rashid, op.cit, n. 42 p.45.
69. Ibid, p.69.
70. *Europa Year Book*, op.cit, n.50, p.1676.
71. 'Migration Trends', *Post Soviet Geography*, (Columbia) April 1993, p.210.
72. Tsuneakisato. 'Economic Reforms in China in the light of Soviet and East European Experiences' in Niiseki ed. *The Soviet Union in Trasition* (Boulder Colorado,) Westview Press, 1987), pp.89-103.

4

Ethnic Identities in Tibet and Kazakhstan

In multi-ethnic states ethnic minorities strive to maintain their distinct identity vis-a-vis other, especially the dominant, ethnic groups. Ethnic identity takes different forms in different social circumstances. It manifests itself in race, language, culture, religion etc. Awareness of the ways in which various ethnic groups are identified as distinct nationalities, is the first crucial step in understanding ethnic relations and ethnic politics. China and the former Soviet Union are no exception to this. Against this background, in this chapter, the two cases under study, Tibet and Kazakhastan are examined in terms of ethnic identities of Tibetans and Kazakhs.

Tibetan Identity

At the heart of Tibet issue lies is a conflict between Chinese and Tibetan ideas of national identity. The barriers to social interaction between the two communities come from the Tibetan side as much as the Chinese. The Tibetans regard the Chinese as outsiders, and have no doubt as to their own distinct identity. This is defined by physical appearance, language, culture, and above all religion. There is no Chinese word for

'Buddhist'. Those who practise Buddhist teachings are nang-pa (insiders). Those who do not are phyi-pa (outsiders)[1] Over the centuries Tibetan national identity became indistinguishable from religious identity and every part of Tibetan society, form the highest to the lowest, was saturated by Buddhist folklore and teachings. Buddhism regulated their lives, their festivals and holidays, their work and their family activities.[2]

The forced incorporation of Tibet into the Chinese empire and the various policies of assimilation and integration failed to signify Tibetans. Chinese communist theoreticians expected ideological enlightenment gradually to override ethnic loyalties, in much the same way as material progress was supposed to remove the need for religious 'superstitions'. However, in practice, the opposite has ensued. The growth of Tibetan national consciousness and reassertion of Tibetan ethnic identity is continuing to take place not inspite of Chinese rule, but because of it. Let us illustrate the various forms of manifestations of Tibetan identity since historic times.

Race

An important fact about Tibetans is the enormous pride they take in their identity. Tibetans, in terms of their racial features, belong to the Mongolian race. Besides this, they are defined by virtue of their belonging to a race whose origins can be traced back toAvolokites-vara, the father of the Tibetan people. Tibetans feel that their race is very ancient and culturally more advanced than the Han-race. Tibetan writers trace their history back to a 'king Srong-Tsan-Gampo who brought the scattered Tibetans under his single rule...with its capital at Lhasa',[3] during 7th century B.C.

The sense of belonging to a particular race represents the existence of a strong and independent Tibet over the centuries.

Language

Language is fundamental aspect of ethnicity. Tibetans have their own language and literature. It was during twelfth century that Tibet acquired its linguistic identity. Tibetan language was codified and writing introduced.[4] This contributed to the creation of a sense of cultural community, introducing some degree of standardization in the use of language. It also produced literate elites empowered to create a new culture on the basis of fixity introduced by writings.[5] Thus, language and literature express not only the "national genius" but also serve a useful purpose in the production of nationalism: a unifying social communication system across the nation. Cultural heroes are ostensibly projected as the towering and inspiring demi-gods of the nationalist pantheon with which mobilised masses can easily and proudly identify, there-by concretizing their sense of national identity.[6]

Directions to use Tibetan as official language have been highlighted in various policy statements. The language policy announced in 1988, calling for Tibetan to become the primary language of official communication within two years, has yet to be implemented and Chinese is still used as the working language in government offices. Tibetans are extremely critical about this issue. Despite having all the attributes of a nation their basic human rights are not protected. They are forced to learn Chinese language for employment opportunities within their native land. Panchen Lama complained in 1988 that "for the past thirty and more years no importance has been attached to the use of the Tibetan language."[7] Many Tibetan resist the idea of learning Chinese in order get along better in their own country, with people whose presence was unwelcome.

Culture

Culture is another important manifestation of ethnic identity. When the Chinese PLA liberated Tibet in 1950, the first reaction of the Lhasa government was not either to defend the territorial integrity of Tibet or to protect natural resources, but the sacred person of the Dalai Lama who symbolized Tibetan culture.[8] Tibetans feel that survival of Tibetan identity depends on Tibetan culture. The value and significance of a culture in turn, depends on the original history of that particular culture. Tibetan culture has firm roots in Buddhism, and is associated with Buddhist traditions and customs. The survival of this culture has been at stake since the Chinese communist invasion of 1950 that aimed at incorporating Tibet into China and destruction of the last vestiges of Tibetan culture. All efforts to suppress cultural values by the Chinese authorities failed. On the other hand, the reform policies helped further strengthen and revive cultural identities of the Tibetans.

Religion

Religion has been most effective preserver of ethnic identities. In case of Tibet, Buddhism played a significant role in defining the ultimate identity of Tibetans. It contains a high tradition of great scholarly sophistication which lends itself to purification, and can constitute the banner of political and spiritual 'Reform' and revival.[9] Tibetans made the bond of religion an important unifying factor for their own nationality.

Since the advent of Buddhism, Tibetan life has been revolving around religion. The Dalai Lama, the spiritual and Temporal head of all Tibetans, has come to personify Tibetan national identity. He is providing the necessary leadership to Tibetan nationalist movement. He remains the most important symbol of Tibetan national unity both within Tibet and among the exile community. The creation of the institution of Dalai Lama dates as far back as 15th Century. Notwithstanding the Chinese occupation of Tibet there is no decline in its importance and influence. Its tremendous force lies in its lofty moral character and the spiritual message it holds for the people of Central Asia.

In recent years religious and cultural forms that define 'Tibetanness' have assumed political significance. Tibetans respond with growing confidence to Chinese attempts to obliterate their past. The rituals of nationalist protest build continuities between the recollected Tibetan past and contemporary political experience. The Jokhang temple in the centre of Lhasa has become the symbolic focus of political protest precisely because it exemplifies these continuities, linking Tibetan identity to its remembered past. The legends of Songtsen-Gampo and the ancient kings likewise reinforce a collective political identity and sustain a sense of political legacy in the face of Chinese political domination. The Dalai Lama as a symbol and rallying point of Tibetan protest exemplifies these continuities, best of all, since he epitomizes both the Tibetan religious and political past and a bridge to the modern world. The sense of constituting a political community is condensed into the figure of the Dalai Lama, who represents not only the pre-1959 government in Lhasa, which continues in exile in India, but a remembered political history stretching back to the time of the ancient kings.[10]

Other non-institutionalized forms of religious expression, such as oracles, divination, and popular cults have the potential for mass mobilisation and assume volatile political forms. Similarly, prayers invoking protector deities to come to the aid of Tibet, as well as the long life payer for the Dalai Lama (rgyal bai Zhabs brtan) and the 'prayer of Truth' (bden smon) written by him, have all acquired an explicit political meaning for Tibetans.[11]

Besides these various forms of religion, a host of non-religious customs that have great practical impact on social life-such as personal names, dietary restrictions, marriage institutions, birth and death rituals, public festivals, even greeting styles and costumes—all of which become additional means of social identification.[12]

To conclude, with the help of several carefully thought policies, Chinese wanted to replace Tibetan identity by a communist ideology in the form of Mao cult. But they failed to eradicate Tibetans' deep religious faith, their sense of cultural identity or their loyalty to The Dalai Lama. In the last four decades very impressive economic, social and cultural developments have taken place in Tibet. Though the Chinese leaders do not recognize, at least in public, it is a fact that development process also stimulates nationalist identities and generates demands for autonomy and independence.

Kazakh Identity

Ethnic identity of Kazakhs is synoymous with their neighbouring Muslim Asian minorities namely Kirghiz, uzbeks, Tajiks, Turkmenians. They are linked by race, religion and tradition to the Islamic countries in the South, than to the Slav dominated Russia in the Northwest. The assertion of the identity of Kazakhs has been latent until recently. Gorbachev's liberalising policies, besides Soviet policies after the revolution, revived ethnic identities. Race/Tribe, language, culture and religion provided the raw material of national identity and served as an integral part of Kazakh nationalism and as crucial factors in its maintenance and growth.

Soviet policies on nationalities tried to suppress all forms of ethnic/national identities through oppressive measures. In this process some of the traditional social structures, mosques, historic places etc. were destroyed but not traditional values attached to those social structures. Kazakhs are known to be most Russified Muslim minorities of Central Asia and least Islamised people. In spite of this, their ethnic loyalties towards Islamic culture and tradition continue to manifest in various forms.

Race/Tribe

Kazakhs consider themselves racially separate from the slavs or Russians and close to the Turkic peoples. They are descended from Mongol and Turkic tribes that settled in the area about the first century BC.They emerged as a distinct ethnic group from a tribal confederation known as Kazakh Orda, which was formed in the late 15th Century A.D.[13]

The Turko-Mongol Kazakh pastoral nomads of the northern-steppe were quite similar to the Kirghiz herdsmen in the mountains to the southeast. But even though their languages were mutually intelligible and inter marriage common, the Kazakhs and Kirghiz maintained distinct tribal structures and their sense of ethnic uniqueness was strengthened over time as each group created its own relations with the various and ever-changing neighbouring powers.[14] Historically speaking; Kazakhstan and Kyrghizia have more in common than other ethnic groups. The age-old admonition in the epic trilogy 'Manas' that "Kazakhs and Kyrghiz are blood brothers", bind them together.[15] The imposed Soviet distinction between steppe dewellers—Kazakhs and mountain dwellers—Kirghiz, has never been accepted by the peoples involved. They strongly feel about their distinct ethnic identity.

Although Kazakh nomads may live for part of year in flats on collective farms, in the mountains they still live in yurts. They stick closely to their clans, refrain from marrying outside the wider tribe and maintain traditions of hospitality and culture that are centuries old.[16]

Language

Kazakh belongs to the kipchak group of Turkic languages all of which belong to the Altaic family.[17]Kazakh was written in Arabic script until the early 1930s when Arabic was supplanted by Latin alphabet. A decade later, as part of the

Russification effort, the Latin alphabet was again replaced by the Cyrillic alphabet. This created deep resentment among Kazakhs. They feel that it is one of the main duties of every Kazakh, every Kazakh family, everyone who regards himself as a Kazakh and the entire population to be proud of their native language, to be concerned for its purity and to promote its development[18] It is, therefore, not surprising that 97.5 per cent Kaza-khs claimed Kazakh as their mother tongue (as per 1979 census). Only 2 per cent regarded Russian as their mother tongue. However, 52.3 per cent of Kazakhs regarded Russian as their second language.[19]

Many newspapers and journals in Kazakh language like *Kazakhistan Ayyelderi* (Women of Kazakhstan), *Madeniyet Zhane Turmys* (Culture and Daily Life), and *Ontuslik Kazakhstan* in particular contain only Kazakh names and the photographs in them largely feature representatives of the indigenous nationality. For them, preservation of native language is tantamount to preserving awareness of their own national identity.

The Soviet authorities, however, felt that this kind of one-sided coverage of life in a multi-national republic tended to artificially consolidated national isolation.Hence, there were always attempts to make Russian the medium of instruction and relegate Kazakh to a secondary position. This attitude towards Kazakh hurt the feeings of the natives. The Kazakhs were dissatisfied with the low priority given to publication of teaching aids in the Kazakh language such as self-instruction books, phrase books and dictionaries of thee Kazakh language. By the mid 1980s, approximately 40 per cent of Kazakh youth were unable to read their native language.[20]

Despite such official efforts to foster Russian language Kazakhs have retained a strong degree of linguistic cohesion. Almost all regard Kazakh as their mother tongue. In September 1989, the Kazakh Supreme Soviet adopted legislation establishing Kazakh as the official language of the republic, while Russian remained a language of inter-ethnic communication.However, all officials communicating with the general public would be required to know both the languages.

Culture

In differing ways and varying degrees ethnic, religious and linguistic forms constitute culture. Kazakhs maintained their underdeveloped culture to assert their identity which is different from the Russian or Slavs. The depth of their attachment to traditional national culture and its religious context remained extraordinarily strong. They have shown a desire to preserve their own characteristics and their own traditions irrespective of the length of the time they have lived under Soviet culture. Seven decades of Soviet rule could not suppress inherent cultural identities of the Kazakh people.

Kazakh culture has pre-Islamic and Islamic elements and aspects of ceremonies in the form of local traditions. All these continue to serve as means of ethnic identity. The leaders are conscious that the assertion of religious roots is an avoidable phase of building a new socio-cultural identity.

Religion

The predominant religion of Kazakhs is Islam, most ethnic Kazakhs, being Sunni-Muslims of the Hanafi School. Islam is embedded in the life of the Kazakhs. It is not only a religion but a way f life. The pervasive presence of religion is all too apparent, especially in traditional festivals, marriage and death rites, inheritance laws, inter personal ethics, primordial outlook on life and world etc.[21]

The impact of Islam is more clearly felt in the countryside, but it is also evident among the urban population, most of them migrated there and retain close ties to relatives remaining in the countryside.[22] Islam served as a force to integrate society, securing its stability and acting as a symbolic expression of ethnic identity.

However, Soviet ant-religious policy has been far less successful in eliminating the more unstructured and informal religion as practised in the countryside, and even in the cities. The type of religious practice that has been preserved is based more on ritual than on doctrine. Religious practices have become more syncretic often infused with local pre-Islmalic rituals, and thus with some justification may be viewed as ethnic or national traditions as much as religious ones.[23]

Sufi brotherhoods played crucial role as preservers of Islam as a faith, a way of life and as an ideology. Atheistic education and mockery of rites and rituals by the Soviet authorities failed to reduce the tenacity of Islam among the Kazakhs. They preserved their historical and cultural monuments and restored mausoleums of religious and quasi-religious figures.[24]

Towards the end of Soviet era, perestroika has radically changed the religious situation in central Asia. Islam now holds a fascination for Kazakhs, not just for religious reasons but because it is part of their historical and national identity which they want to assert and which makes them decisively different from Russians. Until January 1990 Kazakhstan's Muslims were governed by the pliant, Soviet-backed Muslim Religious Board based in Tashkent. However, the ambitious Qazi of Alma-Ata, Radbek Nisanbai, staged a minor coup on 12 January 1990, having himself elected grand mufti of Kazakhstan and setting up his own religious board, independent of Tashkent.[25] Nisanbai opened Kazakhstan's first Madrasah in 1991, published his own translation of the Koran into the Kazakh language and began a monthly Islamic newspaper.At least 250 mosques were built through public subscriptions. "Perestroika had been useful for Islam. Our People now want more Korans, mosques, and Islamic schools. I will give that to them", he said.[26]

In recent years the Kazakhs envisage Islam as a safety-valve not only to reassert their ethnic identities but to define themselves as 'nation'. Contrary to the Soviet predictions that modernisation, assimilation and integration will undermine ethnic identities, these identities are further strengthened with the advent of Gorbachev's perestroika and glasnost. Kazakhs have become more aware of their past history, national heroes, traditions etc which reflect their distinct identity vis-a-vis Russians. Ethnic identities of Kazakhs are taking national form to justify their position as powerful independent nation.

Soviet Union and China which talked about new vision of man during the revolutionary period ended up in imposing the language and culture of the dominant group on reluctant minorities. These processes, in the long run, had a humiliating implication to the minorities' ethnic identity. Nevertheless, liberalisation and democratization revitalized ethnic and national identities. A careful examination of ethnic, identities of Tibetans and Kazakhs tells us that although ethnic identities are functionally similar, subjectively and objectively they exist in different forms—Buddhist or Islamic, Tibetan Or Kaz-akh. The deep faith of Tibetans and Kazakhs in Buddhism and Islam respectively illustrate how religion pervades all aspects of life—social, religious, political etc, and intensifies ethnic and nationalties. The powerful communist institutions failed to eradicate religion which has become a source of strength to re-assert ethnic identities in order to compete for legitimate political power as nations.

The search for ethnic identities in multi-ethnic nations has led to new forms of nationalism. Religious, cultural and linguistic symbols have attained nationalist characters in the conditions of modern world. The two ethnic groups discussed in this chapter. Tibetans and Kazakhs, clearly followed this trend. In the long run, Communist propoganda aimed at assimilation of various nationalities into a single whole Marxist education, anti-splitist campaign and anti-religious policies were carried out accordingly to erase all forms of minority identity. All these efforts proved to be counter-productive.Revival of national identities is taking place in an unprecedented manner. Simultaneously, demands for more autonomy and independence are on the rise. The notions of 'democracy', 'self determination', 'protec-tion of human rights' have become slogans of nationalist demonstrations.

The history of the Tibetans, and their continued resistance to domination by the Chinese as evidenced by popular uprisings (see Chapter V), underground resistance movements and protracted guerrilla activity illustrate the people's extreme and real misidentification with the Chinese people. The enormous pride Tibetans take in their identity is strengthened by the ordeals they have been endured since 1950s. The sense of Tibetans' collective identity can be characterized in ethnic, religious as well as political terms, which is constructed around shared memories. Cultural and historical heroes and king Storng-btsan-sgampo, Ge-Sar are becoming popular in the process of reassertion of national identities. The greater the Chinese struggle to present Tibetans as members of a religious and cultural minority without significant historical or political identity, the more Tibetans adhere to these identities. Some of the most prominent features of renewed ethnic consciousness have taken the form of religious revival, especially, among the followers to Tibetan Lamaism.[27] For example, circumambulation or "Khorra" (bskorba) has a central place in Buddhism. If offers a religious practice without status distinctions, and thus an opportunity to recognize common features shared with other Tibetans from every background and every part of Tibet. In 1987 demonstrations that look place in Lhasa used Khorra as a form of public protest which effectively distinguishes Tibetans from Chinese who do not practice Khorra. By combining Khorra with symbols of Tibetan nationhood the Dalai Lama, the flag—the Drepung monks (who led the demonstration) forged a link between the powerful motivation that underlies religious ritual and the national consciousness that divides Tibetans from Chinese.[28] This monastic protest has an explicitly nationalist content. Tibetan nationalism is very much a modern phenomenon: the thinking of the young monks today has been politicized in a way that could not have been possible in pre-1959 Tibet. Today infact, western political ideas—democracy, human rights etc.—are perceived as compatible with Tibetan nationalism. Western cultural influences which are the result of opening Tibet to tourists, are valued positively by Tibetans, Westerners are generally regarded as allies in the struggle for Tibetan independences.[29] During the last forty years Tibetan Buddhism, which once worked to counter a strong sense of nationality, now works the other way. With the Dalai Lama as its spokesman and with his policy of non-violence, Tibetan Buddhism has come to symbolize Tibet's national identity. Moreover, it is proving an effective ideological counter-balance in the face of the advance of the Chinese brand of Marxism in Tibet.[30] And for Tibetans in exile, Buddhism is rendering immense strength to continue their peaceful struggle for independence.

Tibetan language, too, has been politicized. New linguistic categories are propagating new ideology inside and outside Tibet. While the Chinese tried their best to spread Marxist teachings in Tibetan language, the exile community has developed their own nations about nationalism and patriolism. For example, one of the most freguently used words among the exile community today is 'seems shug' made up of the two morphemes, 'sems' meaning 'mind' and 'shug'meaning 'strengh'. It can be translated as 'love of one's country'. or 'having conviction in the cause'. The cause in question here is (obviously) that of Tibetan independence.[31]

Besides religion, language and culture played equally significant roles in reviving ethnic identities and fostering nationalism. Every form of cultural expression has acquired political importance. Customs that were spontaneously recovered after the end of the Cultural Revolution and the lifting of restriction in the late 1970's and early 1980's are now self-consciously identified with the cause of Tibetan independence and resistance to the Chinese. Folk culture and traditions became vehicles of reassertion of national identities which Tibetans boast of. Tibetans want to estalish themselves as a meaningful demographic and cultural entity. Most nationalist movements began as ethnic aspirations of a group whose bonds were racial, lingustic and culture.[32] Tibetans are no exception to this pheno-nomenon. Tibetans' yearning for recognition 'as nation', in every sense of the term, has found expression in several declarations by the Dalai Lama, symbol of Tibetan nationhood.

In the case of Kazakhs, too, ethnic identities renewed nationalist aspirations. Though Kazakhs are thought to be least Islamised and most russified people, religion acts as a basis on which Kazakh identity rests. Inspite of anti-religious propaganda by the authorities, Kazakh incorporated many elements of religion, and culture into emerging 'national cultures. Today ethnic nationalism is communicated through Islamic symbols. For example, the modern political party, the 'Alash' party of Kazakhstan, [33] uses these symbols to link its campaign to the historic past and to Kazakh nationalism. National awareness is shown by the often heard expression 'you cannot be a Kazakh or Uzbek or Kirghiz without begin a Muslim.'[34] Thus religion is being used as a channel to mobilize people and to assert their distinct national identity as against the Russian and Slavs.

Kazakh's Knowledge of Russian language is the highest among Central Asian Muslims. But almost all of them claim

Kazakh as their mother tongue. They fear that increasing use of Russian would result in a loss of their ethnic identities. Linguistic identities are being adjusted in relation to, or within the framework of Islamic political identity. This kind of formation of an Islamic political consciousness is finding expression in demands for ethnic territory's preservation—'Kazakhstan for Kazakhs'—at various demonstrations. Kazakh's struggle to preserve their national cultures and to save them from extinction is out—spoken. Writers and poets are taking lead in putting forward the national position. The eloquent spokesman of Kazakhs, Olzhas Suleimenov, has advanced this cause before all - union audiences.[35]

It is a fact that Islamic culture, traditions, cultural heroes are honoured as part of their national histories. An attempt is being made to rewrite the period of collectivization. Celebrations of land mark birthdays of previously suppressed figures, such as the Kazakh poet Shakarin, [36] are underway. Every effort to preserve remmnants of historical and cultural monuments, mausoleums of religious and quasi-relgious figures, diereclty or indirectly, is being linked to nationalism and assertion of ethnic identity of Kazahs. Thanks to Gorbachev's policies which permitted this kind of nationalist political behaviour which, though existed prior to 1985, was repressed by the authorities.

Nationalism of Kazakhs and TIbetans adopted several elements from history. culture and religion as marks of ethnic identity. While religion played greater role in case of Tibetan national formation and nationalism, the linkage between religion and nationalism seems to be inevitable for Kazakhs also. 'Islam not only compensates man's weakness, but can also satisfy his needs unconnected with religion: It can help man express himself, to 'find' himself among people, to develop a sense of identification with a nation and its history, to satisfy his needs in social intercourse, and so forth.[37] This phenomenon of resurgence of ethno-religious nationalism and thereby reassertion of ethnic identities is unexpected. Both liberalism and Marxism in their different ways, implied that the attachment to the local and particular would gradually give way to more universalistic and cosmopolitan or international values (Great Han People or New Soviet Men) and identities; that nationalism and ethnicity were archaic forms of attachment—the sorts of thing which would be 'melted away' by the revolutionizing force of modernity.[38] On the contrary, these very processes brought to fruition the particularist tendencies that lay dormant and accelerated the differences of ethnicity and gave them a new direction along state lines. This illustrates that all elements of ethnicity are nationalized.

Symbols and values as means of mobilization instill a high emotional potential in people and serve as a major source for political parties and religious elites in their march toward independent nationhood. Thus, politics of ethnicity create conditions for nationalism. Nationalism never became a great system of ideas, as did liberalism or Marxism. But its influence on politics is even more important then these, if we look at the history of the modern world. Nearly all the wars of the nineteenth and twentieth centuries had their roots in nationalism, and all states now owe their legitimacy to some version of the national idea.[39] In our present context, in the ultimate analysis, nationalism marks the emergence of cohesive social group out of its ethnic womb into the modern political arena. If its political revolution is successful it becomes the nation in charge of the state (as Kazakhstan): if not, it continues its struggle for nationhood and remains an ethnic group (as Tibetans).[40]

Foot Notes:

1. John Bray, "China and Tibet an end to empire?" *World Today*, vol. 46, no. 12, December 1990, p.221.
2, *Tibet the Facts,* a report prepared by the Scientific Buddhist Association for the UNCHR, Tibetan Young Buddhist Association (Dharamshala, 1990), p.10.
3. Denison Ross, 'The Land of the Lamas and its Story' in J.A. Hammerton ed. *An Encyclopedia of Human Races All over the World,* Vol. 7 (Delhi, Gian Publishers, 1985) p. 4919.
4. T. Shakaba, *Tibet: A Political History,* (New York, Potala, 1984), p.25.
5. Georges Dreyfus, 'Cherished Memories, Cherished Communities', article (Spring 1993) Williamstown Mass.
6. Dawa Norbu, *Culture and the Politics of Third World Nationalism,* (London Routledge, 1992) p.69.
7. *Renmin Ribao*, (Beijing) April 4, 1988, pp. 1-3.
8. Dawa Norbu op.cit, n.6, p.208.
9. Heather Stoddard, 'Tibet from Budhism to Communism' *Government and oppositin*, 21 (1), WINTER 1986, p. 76.
10. Ronald D. Schwartz, *Circle of Protest,* (London, Hurst & Co., 1994), p. 221.
11. Ibid. p. 215.
12. Dawa Norbu, op. cit. no. 6, p.69.
13. 'Kazakhastan' Introductory Survey, *The Europa Year Book*, (London, Europa Publications Limited 1994,) p.1675
14. Martha Brill Olcott, 'Central Asia:The Reformers Challenge a Traditional Society' in Lubomyr Hajda and mark Bessinger, *The Nationalities Factor in Soviet Politics and Society*. (Boulder, Colorado, Westview Press, 1990), p.253.
15. Guy G.Imart, Kirghizhia-Kazakhstan: A Hinge or A Fault-Line, *Problems of Communism,* Sept-Oct 1990, p.1.
16. Rashid Ahmed, *The Resurgence of Central Asia:Islam or Nationalism* (London, Zed Books, 1994), p.1-9.
17. Katz ed., *Hand Book of Major Soviet Nationalities* (New York, Free Press, 1975), p.223.
18. *Summary of World Broadcasts,* (SWB)Part I USSR, 14 Fed, 1987.

19. *Current Digest of Soviet Press,* (CDSP), vol.39, no.19, April 1987, p.11.
20 *Kazakhstanya Pravda, June 10, 1989.*
21. Rasheeduddin Khan, 'Central Asia's Geo-political importance', *World Focus*, , Nov-Dec, 1992, p.59.
22. Rasma Karklins, *Ethnic Relations in USSR,* (London, Allen & Unwin, 1986), p.196.
23. Martha Brill, Olcott Op cit, n12, PP.269-270.
24 For example, the Kazakhs have embraced Ahmad Yasawi the first great Turkic Saint, mystic and builder of the Yasawi Sufi order. His tomb is in the town of Turkestan, He is considered as a Kazakh national saint, although the Kazakhs appeared on the historical scene several centuries after his death.
25. Ahmed Rashid, 'Bless Perestroika and send Korans', *Indpendent,* 4, June 1990.
26. Ibid.
27. See Harold Bockman, The Brewing Ethnic Conflict in China', in Kumar Rupesinghe t.al. ed., Ethnicity and Conflict in a Post-Communist World (New York, St Martin Press, 1992), p.92.
28. Ronald D. Schwartz, op.cit, n.10, p.28.
29. Ibid p.92.
30. Samten G. Karmay, 'Identity: Language Ritual and Culture', in Robert Barnett and Shirin Akiner, *Resistance and Reform in Tibet* (London Hurst, & Co, 1994), 0p.114.
31. Tsering W. Shakya, 'Politicization and Tibetan Language', in, Ibid., p.164.
32. Herbert Adams Gibbons, *Nationalism and Internationalism* (New York 1930), p.4.
33. The name dates back to 1917. Alash Orda Kazakh National Party Organized Third All Kazakh National Congress in Orenburg. It proclaimed the autonomy of the Kazakh-Kyrghiz region and set up the Provisional People's Council of Alash-Orda.
34. Marie Broxup, 'Islam in Central Asia since Gorbachev' *Asian Affairs* (London), vol.18, Part 3, October 1987, pp. 283-293.
35. Martha Brill Olcott, op.cit, n.14, p.274.
36. Ibid p. 274.
37. Saidbaev, *Islam i obshchestvo.* 1978). p. 191, quoted in Martha

Bill Olcott, op, . cit, n. 14, p. 271.

38. Hall, Stuart, 'The Question of Cultural Identity' in *Modernity and its Futures*, (Oxford, U.K. Blackwell, 1990), p.312..
39. James G. Kellas, *The Politics of Nationalism and Ethnicity*, (London Macmillan, 1991), p.29.
40. Dawa Norbu, op.cit, n.6, p. 225.

5

Ethnic Conflict in Tibet and kazakhstan in 1980s

Ethnic conflicts and mass demonstrations have intensified in Tibet and Kazakhstan as a by-product of policies of liberalization. The earlier chapters made an attempt to examine nationalities policies, communist reforms, and re-assertion of ethnic identities since communist takeover of Tibet and Kazakhstan. While Chinese policies in Tibet are more repressive than the Soviet policies in Kazakhstan, more or less similar forms of nationalist uprisings in both the cases, especially, during 1980s dragged the attention of scholars on international politics. Tibet witnessed rebellions before 1980 but the events since 1987 took an unprecedented turn. In Kazakhstan, Alma Ata riots in December 1986 heralded ethnic disturbances in Gorbachev era. This chapter will describe the pattern of demonstrations in Tibet and Kazakhstan and their causes and consequences.

Tibet

After the forcible Chinese occupation of Tibet, the first major event occurred in 1959. But the birth of resistance movement against Chinese took place in early 1950s in Eastern Tibet (Kham and Amdo). The events between 1959 and 1979 have not reached the outside world because the Chinese authorities completely closed Tibet until 1979, so that no reporter was able to witness and report on the many anti-Chinese disturbances that did take place. Among later revolts, demonstrations in 1987, 1988 and 1989 received wide publicity. Asia Watch, Amnesty International, Minority Rights Group and many other voluntary agencies published reports based on field studies. Here, we will examine few significant rebellions that took place before and after liberalization and democratization started in China.

1959 Rebellion

This was the first large scale rebellion after Chinese occupation of Tibet in 1950. The background had been set months before the event. B August 1958, the rebel leaders from different parts of Tibet, who had been moving slowly westward toward the holy city, Lhasa, those began actively recruiting within Lhasa itself. Refugees from Kham, too reached Lhasa, along with pilgrims making their annual trek to celebrate the Lunar New Year. A tense atmosphere was created. The rebellion was to follow an invitation to the Dalai Lama to attend a dance performance by the Chinese troops. The venue selected for this happened to be a PLA camp near Lhasa. Since he was preparing himself for a series of forthcoming religious examinations he did not reply. Once again he was asked to fix up a date on which the performance could be arranged. The Dalai Lama agreed to come on the 10th of March. The day before the performance, Kusun Depon, commander of his body guard, was briefed by Brigadier Fu, the military advisor, about arrangements for the Dalai Lama's visit. In an unprecedented manner, the Dalai Lama was asked to reach the camp unescorted by Tibetan troops and the whole affair to be carried in absolute secrecy. Later, the Dalai Lama wrote: "Of course, it was completely impossible for my movements to be kept secret and the very fact that the Chinese wanted to do so shocked my people, who were already greatly concerned about my safety. This news spread like flames on dry grass".[1]

To add to the already tense situation, "a rumour spread at once throughout the city that the Chinese had made a plan to kidnap him. During the evening and night of the 9th of March excitement grew, and by the morning most of the people of Lhasa had decided spontaneously to prevent his visit to the Chinese camp at any cost".[2] On the morning of the 10th people gathered around`norbulingka' (the Dalai Lama's summer place, where he happened to be at the time). The Rebellion was undoubtedly initiated and led by Khampas, Tibet's warrior class, but there were other participants too, including most of the "Tibetan army of only a little more than 3,000 men"[3], most of Lhasa's 20,000 Monks,[4] a great number of 10-30,000 public[5] and of course, the 10000 Khampas[6] who had arrived Lhasa by 1959. Absence of communication network, lack of modern organisation limited the scope of the revolt. Tibetan's staunch belief in the Dalai Lama, personification of Tibetan Buddhism, who the rebels popular support and sympathy.The uninterrupted struggle against most heavy odds for six years more is a testimony to this fact. Generally, in any kind of revolt the rebels demonstrate in front of the rival party. Here was a case where the Tibetans surrounded not the Chinese Head Quarters, but the Dalai Lama's palace as a symbolic gesture to protect and prevent him from visiting the Chinese military camp. Jawaharlal Nehru best summed up the situation when he remarked that the revolt in TIbet was 'more a clash of wills...than a clash of arms'.

Between 13th February and 25th March 1959, momentous events and silly episodes took place in Lhasa, a blow by blow account of which has been written by a British journalist.[7] He writes, "to western eyes, the reaction of Tibetans to these infractions of protocol may seem exaggerated (though one can imagine the hullabaloo in London if an invited diplomat chose to boycott the State Opening of Parliament). But one has to remember that Tibetans had been smarting under occupation for eight years, and if their emotions were exaggerated, then that is what happens when simple, devoutly religious people feel they have been affronted.[8] What was so striking beneath this strange medieval, religious and folkish behaviour was a resolute and fanatical sense of anti-Chinese and anti-Communist feelings.[9] Mass meetings were held in Lhasa and at Norbulingka with the citizens demanding restoration of full independence. The slogans that were shouted had strong overtones of nationalism. "Drive away Chinese'. "Independence for Tibet" etc.[10] The NCNA communique on the revolt scornfully commented that the spirit of these reactionaries soared to the clouds and they were ready to take over the whole universe.

What triggered the violence was an incident that further suggests the anti-Chinese character of the rebellion. Some in the anxious crowd that gathered around the Dalai Lama's palace on 10th March sighted a Tibetan aristocrat-official who was well-known as a Chinese collaborator, and the angry crowd shouted at once: "Chinese Spy!"[11] He was stoned to death. A little later a member of the Kashag (the Dalai Lama's Cabinet) arrived in a Chinese jeep with Chinese escorts. The enraged public started at once pelting stones at the high Tibetan official, but he managed to escape death, thanks to the Chinese jeep.[12]

The Dalai Lama was appalled at this news and to defuse the angry crowd, decided to cancel his visit to the Chinese camp. His officials conveyed the message to the Chinese authorities and the Dalai Lama personally assured them that he would never go to the camp. A this point most of the leaders left and went to the city, where further demonstrations were held. Many of the people still remained outside

Norbulingka.[13] As evening feel, another meeting was held which was attended by about seventy representatives of the Tibetan government, the Dalai Lama's body guard, and rebel leaders. It was resolved to renounce the 17 point Agreement and call for the expulsion of all the Han from Tibet.[14] The Dalai Lama's appeal to his ministers to reduce the tension failed to bring the situation under control. On 17th March the Tibetan rebels sent a telegram, which the Chinese intercepted, to their nationalist organisation that had been operating in Kalimpong in India since the early 1950s. The message read in part:

> The independent country of Tibet was formed on the first day of the second month of the Tibet calender (that is 10 March of universal calender, the day on which the rebellion started—NCNA editor). Please announce this to all...[15]

H.E.Richardson, who spent several years in Lhasa first as a British and then as Indian Resident, writes that one of the most popular ways of expressing public opinion was in songs that people sang.[16] In Lhasa maids who fetched water for the aristocratic official class often sang lampoons about the latest follies of their masters. In the late 1950s the most popular song throughout Tibet was the anonymous verse:

> We would rather have the Dalai Lama than Mao Tse-Tung;
> We would rather have Kashak[17] than U yon Lhan-Khang;[18]
> We would rather have Buddhism than Communism;
> We would rather have Ten-Sung Mag-Mi[19] than the PLA;
> We would rather use our own (wooden) bowls than (Chinese) mugs.[20]

The overall Chinese policy towards political Tibet was undoubtedly realistic and imaginative perhaps based on the United Front Strategy. But with regard to ethnic Tibet the Chinese policy was based on a rigid legality and lack of realism: treat the ethnic Tibetans living in China and twice as numerous as those under the Dalai Lama as both de jure and de facto Chinese since they were not under the jurisdiction of Lhasa. This was one of the fundamental flaws in the Chinese Policy in Tibet and a basic cause of the revolt. It was a great error to base policy on such a sensitive issue on such rigid apparent legality so far removed from the actual situation.[21] For the fact was, in the 1950s, that no mater how far these Eastern Tibetans were away from Lhasa or even how relatively close they were to the Chinese provinces, they behaved and acted like any other Tibetan.[22] The Chinese should have thought over this fact.

As long as the Chinese did not tamper with the objectively functioning social system and the value systems still considered sacred by the members of that society, as happened on Outer Tibet, there was no revolt, although the unprecedented Chinese presence in the Country caused great resentment and anxiety. But the moment the Chinese tried to alter the functioning and sacred social system in Inner Tibet which they considered de jure China proper, the revolt began. Certainly, the Tibetan rebellion was in defence of Tibetan Buddhist values, and the political and sacred institutions found upon such values. To impose revolution on a functioning society is like burying a man alive. In such a case one man's conception of revolution inevitably becomes another man's destruction. Hence, the Tibetan Rebellion.[23]

To a great extent, religion was one of the major causes of the revolt as explained earlier in this chapter. Therefore, some scholars regard the 1959 revolt as essentially "anachronistic" at a time when we are stepping into the Twentyfirst century. But with the kind of pre-modern ideas that prevailed in Tibet during 1950-1959, it was quite natural for Tibetans to experience religion-bound revolt. The Chinese invasion was perceived more as a threat to their faith than a threat to their territorial integrity and the main goal of the resistance movement was the defence of Tibetan Buddhism as personified by the Dalai Lama. The leaders of the revolt, Who were devoutly religious further reinforces the religious nature of the revolt. For example, Andrugstang, the hero of the 1959 revolt, is remembered for his deep devotion to Dharma (i.e Buddhism).

Since the revolt was also against the reforms that the Chinese were trying to introduce, the Chinese officially interpret the revolt one as by the 'upper strata reactionary clique"[24] in order to well establish their position at various levels of the government. But most of them were formally co-opted by the Chinese and the class composition of those who participated in the revolt appeared to cut along religious more than on economic lines. When the Dalai Lama failed to bring normalcy during the revolt, on Oracle's advice, he decided to leave for India. And soon after, at 10 a.m. on 20the March 1959, the PLA command in Tibet was "ordered to take punitive action against the clique of traitors who had committed monstrous crimes". The rebellion was suppressed after ''more than two days of fighting" by the PLA. ''By the end of the first day...the Nor bulingka was deserted smoking ruin full of dead."[25] On 28th March the government of Tibet was dissolved.

No one knows how many were killed in the Lhasa Uprising which was repressed with a savagery reminiscent of the Nazis in Warsaw but the csualities may have been as high a 10,000[26]. Not generally known is the fact that two days after the Uprising had been crushed several thousand Tibetan Women marched through the streets of Lhasa and called for the Chinese to get out of Tibet. There followed mass arrests and many Tibetan women, including most of the leaders,were imprisoned and tortured for years. Public executions followed after but most of those executed were unrecognisable as they had been so severely beaten.[27] A "rough account" by NCNA showed that by 23 March, more than 4,000 "rebel troops were taken prisoners, and 8,000 small arms, 81 light and heavy machine guns, 27 mortars, six mountain guns and 10 million rounds of ammunition were captured", Considering Tibet's total population of 1.2 million, China thought the rebellion by "20,000 people, mostly people who were deceived and intimidated to join in"[28] was not all that significant. But the extent of the popular participation in the rebellion may perhaps be better gauged by the following PLA proclamation which appeals and "hopes" that Tibetan public would not help the rebels:

We hope that all the people in Tibet, Lamas an laity, will energetically help our army in the campaign to put down the rebellion and not shelter bandits, supply the enemy or provide the rebellious bandits with information (emphasis added).[29]

One of the Chinese report claimed that the resistance amounted to no more than 7,000 "rebels" and was put down easily in two days. This view has been contradicted by the Chinese authorities themselves. Chinese intelligence reports admit that the PLA killed 87,000 members of the Tibetan resistance in Lhasa and surrounding areas between Marchand October 1959 alone. (PLA Military District's Political Report, 1960).[30]

A thorough analysis of the revolt makes it clear that it was highly localized confined almost exclusively to Lhasa and the Loka region. One refugee reported that the people of Sakya,an important centre only a few days' travel from Lhasa, only learned of the revolt when the PLA arrived there in April.[31]

After the Lhasa uprising bitter fighting raged throughout Central Tibet with more Khampas engaged in pitched battles with Chinese troops attempting to capture the Dalai Lama, who was heading towards India. Anti-Chinese struggle found its expression at various rebellions after 1959.In 1969/70 during the years of the Cultural Revolution an enormous rebellion occurred in the Southern province of Loka, only to be bloodly repressed by the Chinese and sporadic risings continued well into the 1970s, and began again from 1987 onwards.

Next to Tibet and China,India was the nation most affected by the revolt. A flood of people entered Indian territory and gradually established their government in exile at Dharmasala. This present abode of the Dalai Lama is often refered to as 'Ittle Lhasa'

The 1959 revolt is known for its brutal suppression. It also resulted in few positive developments. In 1959, soon after the insurrection was put down,the Preperatory Committee for the Tibet Autonomous Region (PCART), held a plenary meeting that decided, in line with the people's demands and the directives of the central government, to abolish serfdom and initiate democratic reform in Tibet. [32]As a result, the life styles of Tibetans changed drastically.

The government adopted a policy of redemption toward slave and serf owners and nobles who did not join the armed rebellion. It bought their extra land, farm animals and tools, and distributed them to the ex-serfs and slaves.[33]

On the international level, United Nations passed a resolution calling upon China to respect 'the fundamental human rights of the Tibet people and ...(their) distinctive cultural and religious life'. The resolution was passed by a vote of 49 for 9 against, and 26 abstentions.[34] Prior to this, International Commotion of Jurists (ICJ) established a Legal Inquiry Committee (LIC) to conduct a preliminary investigation as to what had happened in Tibet. The findings, published in July 1959. [35] indicated sufficient evidence to warrant a full scale investigation.

We find many contradictions when we compare Chinese and the Dalai Lama's or Tibetans' accounts of the revolt. It is a naked truth that the Tibetan did show the strength of their nationalist feelings on 10th March and at various later events as well which will be examined now.

Thee 1987 Riots

After Mao's death Deng Xiaoping implemented four modernization policies. Most of them had their repercussions in Tibet as well. In 1979, a new policy of greater religious tolerance resulted in hectic religious activity. For example, reconstruction and restoration of the principle monasteries-began in Tibet. The Chinese leader-ship,however, continued to hope for the elimination of all religions, the opium of the people, at any point of time. The Chinese official press proclaimed:according to Marxism, religion comes under the ideological system of idealism. It is categorically opposed to dialectical materialism and historical materialism'...It cannot be abolished by fiat. It takes patient, meticulous and repeated education over a long period of time to weaken its influence. Religion cannot be completely abolished until the attainment of certain stage of the development of communist society.[36] The Chinese saw no threat to their overall control of the process of relative liberalization due to this policy. But they had neglected to take into account the Tibetan attachment to their religion and their spiritual yearning. Religious practices were on the rise. Monasteries started functioning as religious universities on an infinitely smaller scale[37](as in pre-1959 days) Hu Yaobang's visit increased the pace of reform even further, and called for respect for Tibetan culture and a tax amnesty for Tibetan farmers and nomads.[38] Tourism was encouraged as a key to urban development.

At the end of August 1983, the Chinese began a new bout of repression. Political activists, practioners of Buddhism who have argued for Tibetan independence such as Geshe Lobsang Wangchu were arrested. Many more were executed whom Chinese classified as 'criminals and anti-social'elements.In September 1983, some 370 monks who were attempting to rebuild a part of Garden monastery,destroyed by the Chinese, were surrounded by 1,000 troops, beaten up and thrown into trucks. An old monk and former Abbot, Gyam, tso, was beaten to death. It seems that many of those arrested (the total ran into thousands) were set to labour camps in th north of Tibet from which few have so for returned.[39] However,world-wide protests by human rights organisations. Tibetans abroad and the media condemnation made the Chinese to modify their oppressive policy to some extent.

Nevertheless, arrests continued during the period 1984-86. People were arrested for listening to the cassettes of the Dalai Lama's December 1985 speech at Bodh Gaya. During theese years the tourist influx continued and many of them were caught in the riots in Lhasa in September/October 1987.[40]

Since 1980s the renaissance of religion was the manifestation of another phenomenon that Peking did not fully grasp in time; it reflected a profound revival of Tibetan nationalism. Apparently the Communist leadership was never able to comprehend the hearts of the Tibetans. The arrogance and contempt displayed by so many Chinese cadres and their inability to fathom the soul of the Tibetans were paving the way for another disaster.[41] One more manifestation of ethnic conflict began in September 1987 which was the first major event to take place after 1959 rebellion and during liberalization period. The disturbances in 1987 were also a reaction to the rejection of Dalai Lama's Five-Point Peace Proposal by the Chinese leadership. This proposal was announced while he was on a ten day visit to the U.S.A. The American Congress publicly supported the Dalai Lama's initiative and wrote to the Chinese Premier. China accused American Congress of interfering in her internal problems. In one of the statements the Chinese Foreign Affairs minister expressed strong dissatisfaction with the U.S. government's failure to prevent the Dalai Lamafrom indulging in political activities in the United States. To add fuel to the fire, posters appeared on the walls of Lhasan homes and office buildings. Credible testimony indicates that they were pasted up by foreign tourists. The posters set out the text of resolution adopted on 16 June 1987 by the Human Rights Sub-Commission of the U.S. house of Representatives. China stood accused of violating human rights in Tibet, and in particular it was held responsible for the death of a million Tibetans since 1950.[42]

In the short span of ten days in the autumn of 1987 three demonstrations took place in Lhasa, the Tibetan Capital. the first demonstration took place during the Dalai Lama's ten day visit to the United States starting on 19th September. The Chinese put the blame on the U.S. for instigating the demonstrators. The second demonstration occurred on 1st October coinciding with the Chinese National Day, a public holiday commemorating the birth of the People Republic of China. Its symbolic impact could not have been greater, since it was perceived by the Chinese government as a flagrant public challenge to the "unity of motherland".[43] The last demonstration was held on 6 October.

A new pattern of performance emerged out of these demonstrations and it became the model for protest in Lhasa for future demonstrations. Symbols and rituals made their presence felt at each demonstration to express the long suppressed Tibetan national consciousness and public opposition to Chinese rule... It made clear that Religion in Tibet had survived socialist pressures as it has done in Poland, perhaps in a much stronger form. While in Poland the political movement is headed by Solidarity, in Tibet it is the religious orders, the monks who have led the revolts against Chinese authority.[44] The demonstrations were seen as the biggest outbreak of political violence in China since the Cultural Revolution in the 1960s.[45]

Unlike 1959 rebellion, the 1987 riots were witnessed by many western tourists (who had been there since 1985) who supported the Tibetan cause and raised the issue at several international platforms like the United Nations Organisation.

On 24 September, a huge public trial was organised in Lhasa in which eleven Tibetans received sentences for criminal offenses—two of them were condemned to death 15,000 Tibetan, were compelled to attend the rally by their work units and neighbourhood committees. Leading party officials were present, including the vice-mayor of Lhasa, who used the occasion to lecture the crowd on the need to "preserve unity and stability" and to "adhere to the four cardinal principles.'[46] The four cardinal principles are: (1) the leadership of the Communist Party. (2) the socialist road, (3) Marxism-Leninism-Mao-zedong thought and (4) the dictatorship of the proletariat. The execution probably represented an effort on the part of the Chinese to silence and cow the Tibetans who had continually approached newsmen and tourists, and expressed pro-independence sentiments. If such was indeed the case the strategy backfired disastrously and precipitated the first demonstration which occurred on 27th September[47] around 9 a.m. About 150-200 lay people and 26 monks from Drepung monastery demonstrated in the streets of Lhasa, shouting, "Tibet is independent", "May the Dalai Lama Live Ten Thousand Years", and asking the Chinese to quit Tibet.[48] They completed three circuits of Barkhor, carrying the blue, red, white and yellow flag of free Tibet. Two roaring lions face each other in front of three snow mountains (symbolizing U-Tsang Amdo and Kham) and the Tibetan Buddhist wheel of Law. Then they proceeded towards the offices of the Tibetan Autonomos Region (TAR) government. The demonstration including the monks, westerners, were arrested by the police. The Dalai Lama's office characterized the demonstrators as 'freedom fighters'. The presence of a number of foreigners has forced the New China News Agency to admit the demonstrations.[49] The vice-chairman of the National People's Congress, Ngapo Ngawang Jigme, explained that the trouble makers were an isolated group and were not supported by the public.[50] But this protest by a small group of demonstrators followed a much more dangerous outbreak of large scale violence.

Few days later, on 1st October, the Chinese leadership was to receive another blow.The day was observed as Chinese National Day (thirty-eighth anniversary of the People's Republic). The demonstration began around 9 a.m. by monks belonging to Jokhang Temple, Sera and Nechung monasteries and later jointed by many lay Tibetans, the protesters, like the Drepung monks on 27th September proceeded around the Barkhor carrying Tibetan flags and shouting slogans for Tibetan independence. On the fourth circuit 50-60 people were arrested with some violence and then held inside the police station opposite the Jokhang. Two westerns were also imprisoned, but quickly released. Monks were beaten with shovel and electric stern guns were used. About 2,300 angry Tibetans gathered outside the police station in Barkhor square. The police used every means—stone throwing, AK-47 machine guns, teargas canisters—to disperse the crowds.[51] Six of them killed[52] and many were injured. The Tibetans set some vehicles and the police station on fire. Shooting continued for several hours and the streets in Lhasa were red with blood. Curfew was imposed in Lhasa and police vehicles with wailing sirns patrolled the deserted streets. During the following days convoys of trucks with soldiers armed with automatic weapons and motor cycle-sidecars with tripod-mounted machine-guns paraded through the main streets surrounding th Tibetan section of Lhasa.[53] A Tense atmosphere was created.

Notwithstanding the awe some apparatus of repression, the third demonstration of the series occurred on 6th October

1987. It was a peaceful one but the police showed considerable brutality while making arrests which seemed quite unnecessary to western tourists and observers. It is estimated that about 700 people have been arrested and there are reports that the Chinese charged 330 Yuan for the return of bodies to grieving relatives.[54] Telecommunication with Lhasa was cut off and foreigners and journalists were warned not to trace to Tibet as police tightened security in the Tibetan capital to prevent further anti-Chinese protests.[55]

Infact a demonstration for independence had been planned by the monks on the eve the anniversary of the Chinese takeover Tibet in 1950. (October 7) This time it was the turn of Garden monastery to lead the demonstrators, one of the "three seats" of the gelugpa sect. However, they were unable to arrange transportation into Lhasa, and the arrival of police and political cadres thwarted their plans. People in Lhasa assumed that this demonstration had been only postponed until a suitable occasion, and that the next big demonstration would be initiated by monks from Ganden. They did not get their chance until March 1988, following the Monlam festival.[56]

The three autumn demonstration in 1987 had same pattern. They were organised by monks and joined by lay Tibetans later. Circumambulation or 'Khorra' characterized the beginning of the protest, which came to a halt when police intervened. The ritual significance of Khorra is transplanted into the arena of anti-government and nationalist demonstrations. The rituals, besides Khorra, that form part and parcel of daily life of Tibetans—prostrations, burning bsangs (incense), reciting mani—are not only habitual but also remembered through intuition. Their meaning in terms of religious ideology is thus secondary to the fact of their performance.[57] Since 1980s. Unlike during Cultural Revolution, Tibetans did begin to observe religious ritual publicly. Khorra—along with prostrations, turning prayer-wheels and burning incense is acceptable under the new policy precisely because it appears to be private and personal and does not challenge Chinese authority in any manner. The use of Khorra for political protest by the monks illustrated precisely the limits of Chinese-defined religious freedom. In effect, the monks were forcing the Chinese to strike out at religion by striking out at nationalism. Khorra gave the demonstrations strongest ethnic base. Without any status distinctions its followers are drawn from the largest possible circle from all over Tibet Paradoxically, personal practice of religion along with symbols of nationhood (flags etc.) turned into an event of mass rebellion. The places where demonstrations were held—Barkhor, Jokhang Temple—also signified a symbolic opposition to Chinese territory. The Jokhand temple evokes a multi-layered symbolism of Tibetan nationhood that has resisted the Chinese efforts to represent Tibetan national history as ancillary to the power of the Chinese state.[58]

The official response to the events was published on 12th October by a Chinese press agency Zhanguo Xinwen (China News). On 16th October 1987, Deng Xiaoping publicly acknowledged the events in Tibet for the first time, prior to this, on October 13th the Propaganda Department of the Regional Party issued a notice defining the 'focal point' for the ongoing ideological studies initiated by units throughout the region. The points to be stressed were: first, that the disturbances were 'plotted and instigated by the Dalai clique', secondly, that national unity is vital to the policies of reform, opening up to the outside world and invigorating the domestic economy; and thirdly, the two 'inseparables',; the Han and Tibetan peoples cannot live without each other.[59] These studies were to be carried out at various levels 'incorporating every individual into supersvised study and discussion',[60]

There was no reference to political loyalty or Tibetan independence during these sessions. But gradually efforts were made to identify dissidents. The real test of loyalty was whether Tibetans were prepared to criticize the Dalai Lama. Very soon Tibetans managed to cleverly combine religious and political roles of the Dalai Lama to their advantage. At study sessions they would resist on their right to religious freedom and never criticize the Dalai Lama. At various demonstrations they continued to project the Dalai Lamaas the symbol of Tibetan nationhood. Monks and nuns were also to undergo this ideological training to come to terms with communist principles.

Official Chinese accounts continued to condemn press reports and never acknowledged firing and use of arms by police or the massive human or materials loss during and after the disturbances. They insisted that the injuries were caused when rioteers went so far as to snatch away guns carried by policeman and opened fire at the police and common people.[61] Four months later it was Panchen Lama as Chinese representative admitted that "a number of policemen fired warning shots in the air or ground" and "ricochets" injured or killed people. He also claimed that only one person has been hit and killed directly by a bullet.[62]

While Tibetan were grateful for the presence of western witnesses who brought international attention to the situation in Tibet,the Chinese authorities felt embarrassed and condemned an expelled them for instigating protests. Tibet was officially closed to individual travellers. Once more China intensified social and political controls to stop any unwarranted incidents but in vain.

1988

After a brief lull of five months monastic militancy and popular resistance made their presence felt once again in early 1988 during Monlam festival. By that time the arrested monks in 1987 were released. On 21 January 1988, Beijing reported the release of fifty nine people.[63] Nuns, students, monks did participate in demonstrations of smaller scale before Monlam festival in 1988.[64] Their impact was negligible.

The Monlom festival was instituted by Tsongkhapa, the founder of the Gelugpa sect and overlaid on the Traditional Tibetan New Year celebrations according to the Tibetan lunar calender. Originally, this ritual was to last for three weeks. Monlam, a monastic ritual, was marked by prayers by monks for the well being of the world, sermons to lay Tibetans, which included an annual sermon by the Dalai Lama, and philosophical debates by monks of the highest scholastic order the rank of geshe Iharampa (dge bshes lha ram pa). In addition to some 20,000 monks from the three big Geluga monasteries near Lhasa, tens of thousands of pilgrims from all over Tibet arrived for the celebration doubling the population of Lhasa.[65] The celebration was also an important symbol of new liberal religious policy. For the Chinese it was a good opportunity to convince the outside world and their own population, in particular, that true religious freedom prevailed in Tibet. They thought that the black spots of September and October 1987 would be erased. However, the monks from three great monasteries decided to boycott the festival. Some 150 monks held an alternative meeting in Drepung monastery to hold an unofficial prayer meeting of their own.

The Chinese bribed the monks to attend the Festival but their efforts met with little success.[66] However, they were all prepared to meet another wave of demonstrations. Special anti-riot units were deployed long before the event. Countless meetings were held to educate the monks at monasteries about history of Tibet, patriotic feelings and dangers of separatism. Tibetans were told that "our party policy on the freedom of religious belief has been consistent and correct. This policy will not change just because of the riots." In the same tone the monks were further instructed that they must sct a "good example" and "must on no account do evil, nor must they turn themselves into social outcasts". Special bulletins were broadcasted.[67]

The festival which began on 24 February went on without a major incident till the last day i.e., 5th March, except that one monk from Drepung shouted Tibetan independence slogans but be was stopped by other monks. On the morning of 5th March the concluding procession of Monlam began. The statue of Maitreya (Tibetan: byams pa), the future Buddha was paraded in a circuit around the Barkhor. At the end of the ceremony, instead of dispersing peacefully, some monks went upto the dais, where the officials were sitting, including the Deputy Party Secretary, Raidi, Raidi promised the release of Yulu Dawa Tsering, an incarnate lama who had been arrested for speaking to foreign reporters about independence earlier. Once again this demand was raised. One of the Chinese officials threw a stone at one of the monks who was shouting and told him to shut up. The monk from Garden threw the stone back at the Chinese and it hit the megaphone. An assistant monk named Zambala shouted that Tibet was an independent country and the Chinese should go back. Every one supported him and chante pro-independence slogans. One of the Chinese pointed a pistol at the monks but a middle aged Khampa came forward and was shot in the forehead at point blank range and died immediately. The body was put on a stretcher and large number of people walked towards Barkhor shouting slogans. The Barkhor square rang with their repeated shouts of 'Free Tibet! We want freedom for Tibet! Independence for Tibet! Long live the Dalai Lama!. After this incident, matters swiftly got out of hand and the Chinese began using tear gas and firing into the crowd.[68]

Within a very short span of time many skirmishes occurred

and the holiest Jhokang Temple became a burial ground. The police and soldiers who attacked the monks used clubs with nails and knives attached and this explains the severed hands and fingers that were later found near the entrance to the Jokhang. A run outside the temple was reported by an eyewitness as saying 'Don't you know they're killing monks in there.' The police snatched wrist watches and other personal belongings of the monks. Few young novice monks found hidden in cupboards were beaten and thrown to their deaths through windows. People going to the Jokhang next day found every nook and cranny spattered with blood. They also found lumps of human flesh and items of blood stained clothing and it is believed that at least sixteen monks were killed in this massacre.[69] It seems that when police film of the events in the Jokhang was shown to Tibetan security officers they became so angry that they needed to be disarmed.[70] The Chinese intention of teaching a lesson to the Tibetans and to add to their state of terror resulted in another mass murder. Amnesty International and Asia Watch gave wide coverage to these events and condemned the brutal acts of the Chinese against human rights of Tibetans.

Arrests, torture and interrogation continued for the next several weeks. Monasteries were thoroughly searched for 'counter-revolutionary' documents. The arrested were taken to prisons around Lhasa—Gurtsa, Sangyip and Drapchi. Most of them were released in July. The Central Tibetan Secretariat, Dharmasala stated that about 50 Tibetans died and about 2,500 have been arrested in Lhasa alone. According to the late Panchen Lama around 10,000 demonstrators were present during the disturbances.[71] Apart form known cases of death and imprisonment it was reported that 144 monks were still missing and their whereabouts were unknown.[72] The experiences of the released prisoners included repeated beatings, electric shocks, suspension from ropes and attacks by dogs. They were also forced to appreciate communist ideology during political campaign inside the prison. The constant arrests in Lhasa remind on of the 'disappeared' since it is certain that many will not be seen again and the systematic way in which electric cow prodders disabled the prisoners recalls 'might and fog' technique used in Nazi occupied territories to instill the maximum amount of fear into those arrested and to their grieving relatives.[73]

Despite the horrendous lengths of the Chinese terror in Tibet well-authenticated reports indicate that more demonstrations continued to occur in Lhasa and other parts of Tibet. On April 17, 1988 a demonstration of nuns from the Chubsang nunnery near Lhasa took place followed by another demonstration on May 17, 1988 in front of the Jokhang Temple. The later provoked police intervention in which four people died and a stronger form of tear gas was used upon the protester. Some nuns managed to escape while others were reported to have been arrested and taken away by truck to an unknown destination.[74] Demonstrations by nuns during 1987-89 period had special significance. They were small unannounced, unexpected, and unmistigated. The nuns were also subjected to various forms of brutality during their imprisonment.[75] They refused to confess to crimes during interrogations and reiterated their commitment to Tibetan independence boldly. There were determined to sacrifice themselves regardless of the consequences. Individual nuns did play prominent role in resisting Chinese occupation of Tibet. After 1959, till 1988, organized political activity by nuns was unprecedented.[76] Today they are co-ordinating their protest activity with monks and march side by side in demonstrations.

On 30th May, 1988, 6 monks staged a demonstration, carrying Tibetan flags in front of Jokhang Temple. The Chinese soldiers bound and loaded them into trucks upon which Tibetan children had written the slogans 'free Tibet' and 'Long live His Holiness Dalai Lama'.[77]

Reliable sources reported in early1988 mention unrests in other parts of Tibet, besides Lhasa. In the summer of 1987 Tibetan students demonstrated at the Sining (Xining) National Minorities Institute in Amdo. Chinese authorities reacted immediately to contain further protest. More successful demonstration occurred in the third week of December 1987 by about 300 students of Malho Tru (Malho Autonomous Prefecture) Medical College and this was followed by another demonstration in Rekong, also located in the former Tibetan province of Amdo, now renamed Qinghai by the Chinese. Yet another demonstration look place at Chentsa Hsien National Minority School few days later and Tibetan students chanted slogans demanding independence for Tibet, an end to forced abortions and family planning in Tibet. The significant point about these events is that they occurred outside the area officially designated by the Chinese as the 'Autonomous Region of Tibet' and in areas that are extremely remote. Together, they give some indication of the deep hatred the Tibetans have for the Chinese, and the dimensions of the problem which the Chinese are still unable to solve.[78]

Meanwhile unrest continued in Lhasa with wall posters demanding Tibetan independence,and there are reports that Chinese settlers in Tibet carry handguns and regard it as a 'frontier region', Tourist and Tibetan coming inside and going outside Tibet were subjected to thorough supervision by the Chinese officials. Inspite of these precautions a small pro-independence demonstration was held by about 10 monks in lay clothes who were believed to be from Garden monastery. The day, 27th September, 1988, on which it occurred coincided with the day on which series of disturbances started the previous year. Flags were flown during the day at various parts of Lhasa. Police trucks with prisoners patrolled the city in an effort to discourage any further demonstrations.[79] Lhasa was sealed on 1st October and more security personnel were deployed. A special squadron consisting of some 12,000 soldiers was sent to face any eventuality.[80]

The belligerent attitude of the Chinese officials was expressed in one of the earlier statements by the senior Politburo member in charge of police affairs. Mr. Qiao Shi—when he said "The monks are bad and if I had it my way, there wouldn't be any monks in Tibet, and he called for the `merciless repression' of demonstrations.[81] These ideas were put into practice on 10th December when Chinese fired into unarmed demonstrators in Lhasa. Before this event, on November 23 posters with independence slogans appeared and on 3rd December (Butter Lamp Festival) Tibetans gathered in the square before Jokhang to chant Prayer of Truth. It was composed by the Dalai Lama in 1960.

On the eve of Human Rights Day in 1988, news papers in China had been replete with articles about China's commitment to respect for human rights. In Lhasa too, posters and pamphlets appeared stressing the theme of "human rights" (`groba mi'i thob thang). Tibetans described their protest not merely as a struggle for democracy and independence but as a fight for human rights. The outlook of the younger generation has been politicized in such a way that it would not have been possible so in Tibet before the occupation. Access to western ideas, Chinese education have enlarged their thinking abilities without destroying their affinity to ethnic loyalties. They used communist vocabulary to prop agate their nationalist ideas. The Drepung Manifesto[82] is a clear example to this fact. They started perceiving their struggle against Chinese rule in Tibet as representative of a contemporary world wide movement. For instance in the days preceding the demonstration on December

10, 1988, International Human Rights Day, a political leaflet was circulated informing the people of Lhasa: Today is a day commemorating the struggle for human rights. Therefore, along with appealing to the United Nations and friendly countries in order to restore our just rights, we Tibetans would like to commemorate this day.[83] Chinese government officially acknowledged this day for the first time in 1988. The date had no traditional significance for Tibetans. still its international importance prompted them to stage one more demonstration on 10th December. This protest had a clear intention of creating embarrassment to the Chinese government by linking Tibetan nationalist protest with international issues of democracy and human rights.

The demonstration was led by monks and nuns and supported by lay residents of Lhasa. It was planned on larger scale than previous demonstrations that took place so far. The background was prepared several days in advance. Posters appeared on the walls throughout the Tibetan part of Lhasa a day before and early morning of the day of protest.

The Chinese too were all prepared to meet any disaster. A convoy of twenty trucks carrying about 500 People's Armed Police (PAP) soldiers arrived on the night of 9th December. This time Public Security made it clear that they wanted foreigners out of Lhasa by that date (December 10).[84] Instead of Jokhang, Ramche temple was chosen as the stage for demonstration. The monks felt that it was impossible to assemble near Jokhang with too many soldiers around. But their destination was Jokhang after a procession from Ramoche. All of them were very sure of their death if they appeared before Jokhang. Their determination to reach there suggests that the protest contained a dimension of religious sacrifice.[85] The demonstration was to be absolutely peaceful. Their strict discipline was based on religious motives. To be a martyr meant for them to sacrifice one self for the "sake of all sentient beings".

While the procession was on, the Chinese opened fire on unarmed protesters without any provocation from their side. Many Westerns managed to witness the events. Monks, nuns and innocent people died, several injured. The Chinese reported only one death and thirteen injuries.[86]

On week after, on 18th December about 60 Tibetan students belonging to the Central Nationalities Institute in Beijing demonstrated in Tiananmen square to protest killings on 10 December. A Tibetan student said "we had to express our anger about what happened in Lhasa on December 10" All Tibetans everywhere are angry because the police are killing our people.[87] This became a precursor to the tragic events at the same place in Jun 1989. The last demonstration in 1988 occurred on 30th December by 300 students and teachers from Tibet University.. It was't disrupted by the authorities since it had their tacit approval. They carried banners demanding respect for Tibetan language, culture and religion. But there was no display of symbols of Tibetan independence.

After the 1987 and 1988 disturbances, campaign against splilttism intensified. Political education squads known as 'Work Temas' were set up for this purpose. Further demonstrations in 1989 show that the work teams failed to obliterate nationalist feelings from the minds of Tibetan people.

1989

The year 1989 witnessed one of the most destructive demonstrations in Tibet. The seriousness of this protest is manifested in the declaration of martial law on this region by the Chinese government. The failure of United Front, and of Nationalities policy was once again discussed at political meetings. As far as Tibet is concerned the change in party leadership should be noted here (See Appendix I). As a result of continuing ferment Mr. Wu Jinghua, senior Communist Party leader in Lhsa and

First Party Secretary since 1985 has been replaced by Mr. Hu Jintao. During the Panchen Lama's visit to Tibet in January, he made reference to leftist mistakes at a meeting with party officials. The holding of Monlam in 1989 came up for discussion once again. At a meeting on 28th January Dorje Tsering, head of the TAR government, insisted that "the government's policy remains unchanged towards the ceremony"[88] Beijing, *Xinhua*, in English, 11 December, 1988, in *FBIS*, 12 December 1988:44.

Monks decided not to participate under any circumstances after the unforgetful incident the previous year. The death of the Panchen Lama gave them another valid reason to do so.

Tibetans felt that their sole official representative's death would create more problems for them. Certainly his death had upset the balance of political forces in Tibet: it was a loss to the reformers, and removed an important obstacle to a crack-down on all dissent in Tibet.[89]

When the search for the reincarnation of the Panchen Lama was on, Premier Li Peng authorized the Democratic Management Committee of Tashilumpo to oversee the issue.[90] This caused resentment among Tibetans. They were unhappy with the Chinese interference in their religious legitimacy.

In Lhasa, throughout the winter of 1989 posters appeared several times calling on Tibetans to demonstrate. Few temporary organisations were behind such acts. A poster from the"Association of Tibetan people of the Three Provinces" (chol gsura bod mi'i mthun tshogs) thanked the preserves of the Tibetan race, the great warriors of Tibet university, the Beiijing Nationalities Institute and Lhasa Middle school for demonstrating on 30th December. It appeared around the Barkhor on 18th January and called on all Tibetans to fight with a warrior's heart until freedom is gained.[91] Another leaflet issued by "Independence Uprising Organisation" (rang bstan sger langs thshogs pa) demanded the Tibetans to refrain from the traditional festivities marking the New Year (February 7). It paid homage to those heroes and heroines who sacrificed their lives for the cause of rights of Tibetan people and wished long life for the Dalai Lama.[92]

Small demonstrations continued to occur every now and then. They followed the pattern of previous demonstrations—circuit of Barkhor, display of Tibetan flag, shouting independence slogans. There were no confrontations with the policemen until March 4. The demonstration on 5th March, too, did not differ in any manner from the previous ones. A group of young monks and nuns led the protest. Gradually the number of protesters increased. They were being videotaped by the policemen. As they approached the police station, one of the policeman threw a bottle down at them. A Tibetan youth responded by striking a rock which hit the wall of the building. The policemen opened fire immediately giving no time for the crowd to disperse. Few died and many injured. When the peaceful demonstration turned violent shops belonging to Han Chinese were burnt and looted[93] by the Tibetans and vice versa. This wave of demonstrations continued for the following two days.

On 6th March crowds gathered along Dekyi Sharlam. They attacked Chinese civilians for the first time during a protest in Lhasa and looted shops and burnt goods like the previous day. Several protesters were shot dead by policemen, using automatic weapons. Security forces entered Tibetan homes, shooting and beating the occupants, and making arrests. The last day of demonstration was marked by less enthusiasm. More Troops of PLA arrived and took up positions throughout the centre of Lhasa. The same day, Government announced a decree imposing martial law which continued for more than a year.[94]

According to Tang Daxian a senior Chinese journalist with

access to the highest leaves of government hierarchy, the events of March 1989 reflected the continuing dispute in the Lhasa bureaucracy between hard liners and a second faction linked to the recently deceased Panchen Lama.[95] Tang reports that members of PAP (Peoples Armed Police) disguised as monks and ordinary civilians burnt down a central flag pole near Lhasa and led a raid on a government granary on 5th March. Reports claiming 'foreign hand' in the supply of arms to the rioters appeared.[96] This referred to neighbouring Napal, Russia, the USA Japan.

The Chinese government accused the demonstrators that they were planning for another major uprising on 10th March[97] and justified their gesture of imposing martial law for this reason. However, this martial law ended the monopoly of the PAP over security in Lhasa which now rested in the hands of PLA troops. Assemblies, demonstrations and strikes were banned. Strict vigilance was observed on the identity of people, especially the monks and the nuns who led the demonstrations. Many of them were expelled from the monasteries and nuneries and returned to their families. Unorganized tourists were banned. Organized tourist agencies were to be accompanied by Chinese guides. Their movements were closely watched. In short, martial law tried to eliminate dissidents from every nook and corner of the region.

During these disturbances the presence of many foreigners as witness and few as demonstrators was very distressing to the Chinese. Many parliaments raised this issue during discussions and condemned the Chinese for violating human rights. A report by John Ackerly and Blake Kerr (1989) based on personal interviews with Tibetan men and women concludes 'there can be no doubt that the use of arrest, imprisonment and torture of large numbers of Tibetans continues to be an integral part of China's effort to suppress Tibetan Nationalism.[98] China signed the UN Convention Against Torture in December 1986 and the Chinese Criminal law (clause 163) forbids use of torture in prison and provides labor and re-education as means of reforming the prisoners. The evidences clearly show that China violated these norms frequently while treating Tibetan people. Besides, China has not signed the Universal Declaration of Human Rights formulated on December 10, 1948.

The ethnic disturbances can be better understood in the context of on going ethnic national movements in many parts of the world, especially, in the neighbouring Soviet Union which is the biggest communist regime with different ethnic minority nationalities. The expressions of protest confirm and sharpen the social and symbolic opposition between Tibetans and Chinese. They may be considered as steps in nation building exercises. Strict communist controls when combined with relative liberalization and modernization provide new methods for politicizing the old or traditional values. In case of Tibet, this kind of politicization highly succeeded in expressing nationalist feelings and demands for independence as an ethnic entity which is different from China in every aspect.

After the Tiananmen Square massacre in June 1989, the brutality of the Chinese government became more explicit. During this pro-democracy movement thousands of Chinese students died. They too were branded as 'counter-revolutionaries', like the Tibetans. The unrest in Tibet continues till date. Pro-independence demonstrations take place very frequently. Tibetan's deep faith in the Dalai Lama and Buddhism proves to be their greatest strength in the on-going struggle for independence since 1959.

The uniqueness of mass demonstrations in Tibet since 1987 is that they are being led by monks and nuns. This rare phenomenon may be attributed to the Spiritual-Temporal leadership of Tibet since ancient times. Another remarkable feature to be noted here is holy places as demonstration sites. The occurrence of demonstrations in and around religious sites illustrates Tibetans' deep faith in religion and religious practices. Planning demonstrations on particular days of religions, cultural or historical importance further shows how these factors of ethnicity played a crucial role in expressing nationalist feelings. We may conclude that ethnic conflict in Tibet is characterized by a peculiar form of ethno-cultural oriented nationalism with a religious basis, unique among the national liberation movements of the colonial period.

Kazakhstan

Prior to Kazakhstan's incorporation into the Soviet Union, ethnic national movements were suppressed. Kazakhs did participate in Bashmachi revolt (1917-34) along with other nationalities for separate national government. However, this movement was severely crushed by the Red Guards Army. When Kazakhstan was to become part of the Soviet Union `national-self determination' with a right to secede was promised. Later, the Soviet regime suppressed all forms of 'local nationalism. The Kazakhs and other Muslim nationalities resented various policies aimed at destroying ethnic cultures and religious traditions. But their feelings remained unexpressed.

With the advent of drastic changes took place at various levels of Soviet public life. His reformist policies-Perestroika and glasnost-aimed at political and socio-ecomic restructuring. They led to unexpected revival of ethnic nationalism throughout the country. Kazakhstan was the first republic to witness this dramatic change. Few important cases of ethnic riots since 1989, Alma-Ata riots, Novy Uzen disturbances, need specialmention among others.

Alma-Ata Riots

The period from 1986-91 may be characterized as an era of

democratization and national revival in the history of Kazakhastan. The first ethnic conflict was recorded in Alma-Ata, and its ethnic tremors were felt by other republics of Soviet Central Asia and the Soviet Union soon after.

Violent nationalist riots erupted in Alma-Ata, the capital city of Kazakhstan on 17th and 18th December 1986 Gorbachev's purge of Communist Party of Kazakhstan (CPKZ) was the immediate cause of the disturbances. Dinmukhamed Kunayev, the first secretary of CPKZ was known for his rampant corruption and nepotism. Gorbachev sacked Kunayev in December 1986 and replaced him by an ethnic chuvash from Russia, Gennady Kolbin. He didn't imagine the grave consequences of this action until 17th December. Riots broke out on that day in Alma-Ata and continued for for two days. They spread to twelve other cities in the republic.[99]

The Kazakhs felt that Kunayev's removal was an result to the entire Kazakh people, it was seen by certain young people as a blow to their national self-esteem and pride, as a personal tragedy and as a collapse of their hopes. While the Kazakhs were unhappy about the appointment of Kolbin, the Russians congratulated each other,saying "Finally there will be order, these Kazakhs are everywhere—in the institutes they occupy the best posts and are the first in line for apartments"[100] Kunayev's leadership from 1964 onwards was marked by a rise in the national consciousness among Kazakhs, bias toward Kazakh officials, open participation by officials in religions ceremonies. He appears to have been something of a paternal figure in his republic. Although his removal was very much expected, the manner in which the whole process took place hurt their nationalist feelings.[101] The practice of appointing representatives of ethnic groups at the provincial level with Moscow's representatives immediately next to them was followed by the Soviet leader's consistently. For the first time the selection of Russian to number one position triggered a series of demonstrations, first in the capital and later in other towns and provinces of the republic. The departure from the established practice as a means of direct central intervention in the Kazakh republic led to unintended consequences. Soviet television reported on 10th January that a Kazakh, Kubashev, had been appointed as second secretary in an apparent move to dampen criticism,.[102] But the news failed to stop the wave of demonstrations.

On the day of the famous demostration posters appeared near educational institutes and near students' hostels about a meeting in Brezhnev Square. Few unidentified men demanded that the students' must attend the meeting without fail. Thousands of disenchanted young Kazakhs gathered in Brezhnev square to voice their discontent with Moscow's decision to appoint an outside to head the CPKZ.[103] The demonstration appeared peaceful for sometime. Placards were carried with quotes from Leninist Nationalities policies and with the slogans "Kazakhstan must belong to the Kazakhs" "Kolbin Go back to Russia", "Autonomy and separate seat for Kazakhstan at the UN", "We want to join China", America is with us", "Russia is against us", They also sang national songs. few Russians came to watch them.

The Chairman of the Soviet ministers of Kazakhstan appeared before the crowd and, having, named all the state posts occupied by Kazakhs said: "What are you unhappy about ? Which of your rights have been violated ? He immediately ordered everyone to go home. The demonstrators replied that key posts in the army, MVD (Ministery of Internal Affairs)and KGB (Intelligence Agency) of Kazakhstan were occupied by Russians and they refused to disperse. Leaders of the Komsomol repeated similar calls to disperse but without effect.

According to The Guardian, at the peak of the anti-Russian demonstrations there were more than 300,000 people on the streets of Alma-Ata (a city of only a million). It was shocking to the militia who had not been trained to control an ethnic riot. By evening some of them left. The remaining crowd organized a "sit down" in the square in front of the Central Committee of the Kazakhstan Communist Party building in Brezhnev Square.[104]

Violence started when the fire brigade started spraying water to scatter the demonstrators. One of the vehicles crushed a girl who was sitting down and the infuriated people set it on fire. They began to break off the facing from and around the square and throwing them at soldiers and the militia. The response came quickly. The students were beaten with truncheons and kicked and were taken away to the militia station. Few witnesses said they were dumped beyond the town. The soldiers rushed to hostels to beat the students. Some students who showed resistance were thrown out of the windows.

The demonstration, began by the students, was later joined by young workers. Two days later Tass admitted that disturbances occurred in Alma-Ata by nationalist elements. The unlawful action by hooligan parasites resulted in the destruction of public and private property. The authorities condemned the riots as totally unwarranted actions and declared and adoption of strict measures against the instigators to restore complete order in the city.[105]

The western correspondents' reports of the incident expressed more seriousness than those by the authorities, However, both admitted deaths and injuries of several people. One of the most detailed accounts appeared in *The Guardian* (30 December) which was heavily criticized by TASS seven days later as sensational and merely an excuse"to have a go at us if they can. According to the Guardian more than 200 people were seriously injured in Alma-Ata hospitals, and two of the temporary prison camps, used to accommodate drunkards, had been cleared to make room for the 1000 arrested rioteers. The violence was so intense that Russians in the city were told over the radio to stay off the streets on the second day. A Russian woman living in Alma-Ata, was reported saying. "The Kazakhs were coming in from the country side, commandeering buses. Some bus drivers were killed when they tried to keep the mob out of their buses. The rioteers had building materials…and one bus driver was bludgeoned to death with scaffolding poles." She thought the demonstrators seemed very well organized. Some of them brought vodka, cigarettes that had been laced with drugs in a vehicle from the countryside and distributed to the people around. The rioters attacked at least one kindergarten where Russia Children were killed.

During their wild display of nationalism wild rowdies armed with metal rods,sticks and stones beat up and insulted citizens (i.e.Russians). They overturned cars and set fire to them and broke the glasses in stores and other public buildings[106]

Several days later the names of the demonstrators were announced. There was an inquiry in all hospitals and polyclinics with the purpose of discovering who had applied for medical help. The demonstrations had been filmed and used to identify the rioteers. A famous poet Olzas Suleimenov approached the cordon of militaia and soldiers with a request not to touch young people and told them that the youth would find solutions themselves. He, alongwith a Kazakh film Director, had been arrested.Later, he demanded that Moscow Should investigate the Alma-Ata riots because they were a national tragedy,as greet as the 9th April 1989 attack in Tblisi.[107] This shows the seriousness of the events that took place in Kazakhstan in December 1986.

According to some reports, separate outbreaks in the neighbouring towns were also equally violent. Kazakhs who were traveling.

To Alma-Ata in order to join the demonstration were pulled off the trains. Contacts with the worst hit town was broken. Troops were hurriedly brought in to control the situation. Martial Law was declared until the demonstration subsided. The death included three members from the security forces besides several injuries, Chimkent and Jambul were the two towns which remained under martial law till the end of 1987. It was said that Kolbin rang to Gorbachev twice. Gorbachev replied "It is not possible"[108] Soviet leaders were stunned by the sudden outburst of nationalist emotions which led to rethinking of Soviet Nationalities Policy. According to the inhabitants in and around Alma-Ata, as result of various demonstrations, 2138 people were arrested, 280 students were killed and 29 from the cordon of militia and soldiers also reported to have died. Many security personnel and innocent people were hospitalized. Four hundred Russians also supposed to have participated in the demonstrations. A report was circulated among the population by the MVD which put the number of arrested at 280 and admitted only one death in order to sound convincing the report pointed out that many of the demonstrators did not have relatives in Alma-Ata.The dead were buried outside Alma-Ata.

The tension continued for few more days with unlawful acts by gangs of hooligans. Some of them appeared beating up everyone they came across. After these events the Russians commented: What is needed is a machine gun to kill at (Kazakhs)" They should be sent to Urals (mountainous region), Alma-Ata should be cleansed of them.[109]

The demonstrations were organised and carried out, with the apparent support of local Kazakh officials, Kazakh university students and faculty members resentful of the appointment of a Russian as first secretary and fearful of an attempt to reduce the number of elite positions in the local party and state bureaucracies available to them. The Kazakh officials later admitted that the nationalist riots were larger, more widely supported and more violently suppressed than was officially reported at that time. To contain further unrest, no official figures for causalities or damage had been published immediately.

The ethnic clashes which made anti-Russian sentiments obvious, clearly taught a lesson to the Soviet leaders. This Violent expressions of popular dissatisfaction with Moscow's policies, especially among the younger generation was but a forerunner of more ethnic conflicts to come within the Kazakh republic (Novy Uzen disturbances which we will discuss in the following section) and in many other republics of the Soviet Union. Anti-Russian feelings were manifested time and again at various demonstrations.

The causes of ethnic conflict in Kazakhstan are varied. Official sources said: discontent with the existing system, uncertaininty about future, a feeling of deprivation, dogmatism, selection and planning of cadres, favoritism, alienation from real life instead of an active internationalist policy-both in education and in the distribution of benefit—are the reasons for nationalist disturbances. According to a Kazakh writer, "bribery, corruption, servility, personality cult, absence of criticism and self-criticism, parasitism, careerism and deception, failure of the authorities to wage a persistent struggle against hooliganism, alcoholism and drug-addiction, especially among the juveniles,"[110] induced the riots. It is generally agreed that the local Soviet authorities' treatment of the crowds on 17th December, 1986 was harsh and led to a violent repression of the Kazakhs who tried to give vent to their political aspirations[111] with a nationalist touch.

The Kazakh authorities set up a commission to inquire into the disturbances in Alma-Ata. This commission also concluded that the official version of the December events differed in many respects from what actually occurred. The Commission emphasized particularly that the demonstrators were not a bunch of "alcoholics and drug addicts" but a politically and socially aware group of young members of the indienous population. it stated; "the underlying causes of the young people's dissatisfaction were the lower standard of living, social injustice and the failings of the command administrative system."[112] The commission's findings confirmed instances of brutal treatment of demonstrators and use of unconstitutional methods. It proposed that 17th December be designated as a memorial day or a day of 'democratic renewal' in memory of the tragic events of December 1986.[113] And this day has now been declared as 'National Day' by the newly independent state of Kazakhstan.

However, some measures were taken to eliminate the 'nationalist' elements as far as possible. Restructuring took place at all levels. Kolbin reacted sharply, singling out the Communist youth League for a severe purge, saying repeatedly that his move was not aimed solely at the Kazakh members—a statement received with scepticism by native population. He also stepped up action against those who were found participating in religious ceremonies or rituals. Said Aqa Ziayev, the head of the party in Jambul province, was sacked for a public show of respect for religious sites. Later, another party official was accused of diverting public finances for the construction of an unauthorised mosque.[114] The publicity given to these incidents further inflamed Kazakh susceptibilities. Hostel facilities were improved to placate students. Many senior university officials, who were among the leaders of the riots, were detained. Articles appeared in leading journals which called for education to provide people with a "firm world outlook" which meant communist world outlook. Official sources admitted that informal gangs were allowed to get away with accosting and beating up Russian students on many occasions.[115] Serious discussions were held at party meetings and higher education establishments about overcoming nationalism in the republic. Mass media were instructed to step up the propagation of the Leninist nationality policy and to demonstrate graphically and profoundly the meits of Soviet way of life and thc friendship of Soviet peoples. Visits by Western reporters tọ Alma-Ata were canceled considering the tense situation. Security personnel were instructed to protect the rights of citizens in accordance with socialist law at the same time to punish anti-social elements severely. A resolution was passed by the Kazakh Party in this regard. It also aimed to wage a struggle against negative phenomena—alcoholism, parasitism and non-labour incomes.

Efforts were made to reduce inequalities between Russians and the Kazakhs. A broad programme to improve the supply of food stuffs was planned. (Food shortages were thought to have played some role in fueling riots). Those who aroused unaware young people with demagogic slogans and appeals, drew them into fights, riots and acts of arson and incited them to commit outsages, were given death sentence. Arrests continued to take place whenever instigators were identified. A thorough re-evaluati of Soviet nationalities policy took place.

All these measures were taken after carefully considering the realities reported after Kolbin and Mikhail Solomentsev (a member of Politburo and Chairmen of the Party Central Committee) toured various parts of republics.[116] They held meetings with professors, Komsomol organizers and other imporant officials who run the administration of the republic. Resolutions were passed to improve the instruction of Kazakh as well as Russian languages is schools. Kolbin showed extreme sensitivity towards Kazakhs throughout his tenure as first secretary of the republic. At a meeting of the Central Committee of the Kazakh Communist Party on nationality relations Kolbin admitted: "It would be an error to consider that the national processes which are taking place are without their problems." To reduce inequalities he also called for a fair national representation in the party and government bodies and a fair enrollment of young people of various nationalities in higher education establishments.[117] The need to develop the activities of Party, Trade Union, Young Communist League in the light of 'unhealthy manifestation' of December events was reiterated. Education of Young men and women on international lines was considered to be the immediate task in order to deepen the fraternal ties with other republics of the Soviet Union.[118] A co-ordination council was set up to fight negative phenomenon is the republic—protectionism, nepotism, clannishness, bribery and abuse of official power.[119] In short, change on radical lines was started to end stagnation and inertia in the republic.

The events in Kazakhstan forced Gorbachev to give considerable attention to the hitherto neglected aspect of his policy—nationalities relations. Only a month after the Alma-Ata events,in a report to the January 1987 plenum of Central Committee, he conceded that national feelings deserve "respect", and hat policies affecting nationality relations required" special tact and care". He stressed the need to combat negative phenomenon which manifested in incidents similar to those which look place in Alma-Ata. Gorbachev thought "the event in Alma-Ata called for serious analysis", and "a principled assignment for enhancing internationalist education" especially with a view to "save the rising generation from the demoralizing effect of narrow nationalism". In June 1987 plenum he included ethnic group interests among those he defined as interests that would have to be taken into account in the policy making process. Once again, in his report to the February 1988 plenum, he elevated the national question to an issue of "vital" importance.[120] Thus as ethnic riots increased in number and intensity, Gorbachev' outright indifference to the ethnic dimension of Soviet politics came to an end. An open concern to respond to ethnic sensitivities is expressed at various important meetings.

While drastic changes were being implemented at official, levels, by 1988 various informal groups had provided an opportunity for ordinary citizens to become involved in political action. Main concern of these groups had been environment or language issues. Few of them had a particular political and economic significance in Kazakhstan for example, committees set up by striking miners in Karaganda oblast in 18th June 1990.[121] Other groups included Alma-Ata Popular Front/Democratic Union, Alash, Nevada Semipalatinsk Adilet, Islam and Democracy, Atmakeen etc. A deputy Republican Prosecutor reported the existence of more than 300 informal groups with more than 3000 members. They played effective role in moving bureaucracy to take action to reduce tensions in ethnic relations.[122] However, the authorities in Kazakhstan were strongly opposed to these groups and tried to repress them or co-opt them.

Kolbin made every effort to increase the cultural autonomy of Kazakhs and overhaul the party apparatus gradually. His policies were more supportive of Kazakh interests than what his appointment seemed to portend, Moscow's instruction.

Moscow's instruction combined with Kolbin's serious ways to stop ethnic conflict in the republic were not totally successful. He had lost the support of the CPKZ and was defeated in the election of March 1989, being replaced by Nursultan Nazarbayev. The new leader consistently supported Moscow's reforms. At the same time made sincere efforts to represent the aspirations of Kazakh people. To this end, the party changed its position on a number of key issues to retain it authority over the population and thus tried to project a new image. Fresh steps began to be taken for (a) making Kazakh the state language in the republic (b) eliminating the blank pages of Kazakh history, (c) preserving the republic's natural resources, and (d) brining economic autonomy for Kazakhstan.

Despite these efforts Nazerbayev did witness ethnic clashes during his tenure as the First Secretary of the CPKZ. 'Novy-Uzen Disturbances' is a case inpoint.

Novey Uzen Disturbances

In June 1989 ethnic riots took place at Novey Uzen city in the Guryev province of Kazakh republic. After a brief spell of peace after the Alma-Ata riots, the Novy Uzen disturbances caused concern to authorities once again. The population of Novy Uzen consists of approximately 56,000 people, including about 20,000 who are representatives of peoples of Caucasus: Armenians, Azerbaijanis, Lezghians and others. The city's life is characterised by high prices, inadequate housing, unemployment problem, poor social conditions, malfunctioning of cooperatives etc.

The disturbances began on the night of 16th June 1989 touching off a wave of riots. On the evening of 16th June, a fight broke out on a dance floor between groups of indigenous and Caucasian nationalities.[123] Anti social activities were carried, out,public property was damaged, and even homes were not spared. During the disturbances iron bars, clubs and stones were used unsparingly. Public services—policies station, water supply system etc.—were paralysed and many establishments were shut down causing inconvenience to normal life. Many people were injured and a few died. Use of fire arms and inflammable materials was also noted. Many demonstrations and rallies were held in front of Party Committee and Soviet Executive Committee buildings. The number of protesters at various places ranged between 250 to 7,000 Women and children also participated. Their posters and slogans, written in

Russian and Kazakh, said: "We demand a fair distribution of benefits!" 'Equal work, fair distribution of income!' and "Young people want work!" When the party Republican authorities visited the scene, four demands were placed before them: (i) release of the people detained for hooliganism during the mass disturbances, (ii) handing over of the head of the Novy Uzen city internal affairs department for a settling of scores. (iii) Expulsion of every member of Caucasian nationality from the city within seven days and closure of their cooperatives, and (iv), to find jobs for all the knee of indigenous nationality.[124] Many Troops were deployed to restore law and order.

Following the violent disturbances, several hundred people of the Caucasian nationality were taken outside the city limits, where they were given protection by police officers and USSR Ministry of Internal Affairs troops and provided with food. Later they were returned to their own homes. An operational head quarter was set up to co-ordinate the activities that were underway. Curfew was imposed to control the situation. It was also reported that many Caucasian nationals left Novy Uzen.[125]

Soon after, the violence spread to nighbouring provinces from June 22 to June 23, 1989 where there was no curfew and patrolling. Dzhetybai, Munaishy, and Yeraliev witnessed mass disturbances. Later, it came to notice that the persons detained were residents of Novy Uzen. They apparently came from there especially to organize demonstrations. Rumors were floated to stir the people in Tselinograd, Semipalatinsk, Kokchetav Pavlodar, Kustanai and Chimkent Provinces,[126] including Kulsary, Shepke, Mangyshlak and the town fort of Shevchenko. In Kzyl-orda, some 30 taxi drivers left the depot and drove around the city trying to assemble people for a rally. Dzhambul province and several others areas witnessed the appearance of inflammatory leaflets of nationalist content with calls for disturbances. As a result of these ethnic clashes, 5 government vehicles, 9 consumer service enterprises, 13 co-operative establishments, 18 small retail shops were damaged of a total 5 have died since June 17th, and more than 20 hospitalized. A total of 3,516 people have left for Caucasus.[127]

The events in Novy Uzen depict that Central Asian nationalism has not been only Islamic in nature. It has a number of other components. It has long been and remains today, on the whole, xenophobic, above all anti-Russian has become quite clear.[128] in this case. The Kazakhs turned against unidentified Caucasians who had allegedly been given both homes and work at the expense of the indigenous population, by the Soviet authorities. Poor, social conditions, high prices prevailed. The failure of Party, Soviet and Law enforcement agencies, to intervene in favour of local Kazakhs also caused these people to distrust them. This in turn ripened the conflict that exploded in Novy Uzen in such an outburst of emotions.[129] After the tension had finally subsided life became normal. An organisation, made up of Caucasians emerged spontaneously. It came to an agreement with the Birlik Committee, created by Kazakhs to tackle the social and national-cultural problems together.[130]

Though the conflicts in both Alma-Ata and Novy Uzen, clearly manifested the anti-Russian sentiments, they differed from each other to a great extent. In the case of Alma-Ata, the major cause was the removal of a Kazakh and his replacement by an ethnic Russian as First Secretary of the Communist Party which was a deviation from the general practice. An examination of the reasons for the Novy Uzen disturbances reveals that the low standard of living of the Kazakh and their antagonism towards the Caucasians appeared to be the main cause. The riots in Kazakhstan brought to limelight the failures of Soviet nationalities policy. It demonstrated the strong presence of nationalism as an undercurrent within the non-Russian Communist Parties themselves. The riots also exposed the emotions of non-Russian nationalities, which were given a ventilation by Perestroika and glasnost. Such sentiments echoed both within and outside the republic. Within Kazakhstan, Uralsk, Temirtov, Karanganda oblast and Novy Uzen city experienced mass disturbances. According to an Alma-Ata Radio report, "these violations of public order are due to the low standard of educational work in work collectives, and the inadequate influence of Komsomol and other public organisations on young people."[131] Outside the republic similar events occurred in the neighbouring Central Asian Muslim republics of Uzbekistan, Kyrghizistan and Tadzhikstan.

However, it came as a surprise that Kazakhstan, of all the Central Asian republics, was the first one to experience such a violent outburst of discontent and nationalism, even though the Kazakhs were generally believed to have the highest degree of Russification of the Central Asian Muslim republics. These events demonstrated the hollowness of the Soviet claims of the nationalities policy.[132]

Despite Nazarbayev's meticulous measures, ethnic disturbances did take place again. In June 1990 following an incident in Temirtav involving Azerbaijani and Kazakh students which resulted in the death of two of the students, there were fresh attempts to fuel the conflict after rumours had lent the incident an inter-ethnic hue. There was also unrest between Kazakhs and Chechens. Again in September 1990 a citywide rally took place in Alma-Ata in the Square in front of the building of the Presidium of the Kazakh Academy of Sciences. Several hundreds gathered carrying banners written in Kazakh and Russian. "We will not give up an inch of Kazakhstan's land!" "We will not let Kazakshtan Be Torn Apart", "My People, Prepare to Defend you land, "Turkestanfor the Turks", "Expel Chauvinists—Goloko, Vasilyeva, Petrushenk (USSR people's deputies from Eastern Kazakhstan oblast) from Kazakhstan", as they were charged of campaigning for the transfer of Eastern Kazakhstan to the Russian Federation. One more incident took place in October 1990 in Alma-Ata. Speech delivered for more radical measures to achieve Kazakhstan's real sovereignty were heard by young people, and leaflets were also distributed.

The Ethnic riots in Kazakhstan are significant for the fact that violent ethnic disturbance with nationalist overtones occurred in an era of increasing perestroika and glasnost. Kazakhs, though a minority in their own republic had the potential to organize demonstrations and express their suppressed feelings of nationalism. Thanks to Gorbachev's liberalizing policies. These policies aimed at political and economic reforms, in turn, produced ethnic nationalism. The deceptive success of Soviet Nationlities policy has shown its true colors. It is to be noted that nationlist feelings did not emerge all of a sudden. They were nurtured throughout the communist era with the help of religion, culture and other fundamental aspects of ethnicity. Only that these feelings found expressions under Gorbachev's leadership seems remarkable. Nationalities Question has played greater part in Gorbachev's life as the leader of the biggest communist regime in the world till the end of his tenure (*i.e.* August coup in 1991)

However, if plans for decetralization in decision-making are to accompany the proposed economic reforms, this is likely to encourage nationalist aspirations[133] and threaten the unity and integrity of a multi-national state. The riots in Kazakhstan clearly show that nationelism is often present in non-Russian nationelities. In addition, calls for more emphasis on internationelist education (*i.e.*,a thinly disguised russification whose primary goal is anti-religious Propaganda or atheistic education) could have the opposite effect to that intended, creating further discontent.

The aftermath of the riots in Kazakhstan was crystal clear.

The'National Question' overshadowed socialist principles of the Communist Party programme and major policy agendas.The sudden outburst of violent nationelist expressions represented a qualitatively new challenge for the Soviet leadership. Gorbachev's serious concern for national relations led to greater controls to contain 'national' or 'local'chauvinism. The ethnic conflicts exposed the limits of 'glanost'. When more disturbances occurred on similar lines in other republics the whole country found itself caught in an ethnik trap.Eventually, the Soviet empire disintegrated soon.

More than four—and a half decades of Chinese rule in Tibet and seven-and a half decades of Soviet rule in Kazakhstan were unseccessful in erasing religion (which is the 'opium' of people according to Marx)from the minds of these ethnic minorities. Every sphere of social, political, religious life underwent Sinicization or Russification. This process did not spare even the names and places of residence of these peoples. Despite these facts, the conflicts in Tibet and Kazakhstan illustrate that Marxism-Leninism were over powered by ethno-nationlism and ethno-cultural values which carried spiritual and moral messages. The persistence of ethnic conflicts proved that Marxist principles could not provide a just alternative to these values. Besides serving as moral and spiritual guide, religion strengthened ethnic loyalties and community feelings. Over the years, these feelings were nationalized and mobilized people to struggle for a common goal-real autonomy which is tantamount to independence. This is evident in both the cases under study—Tibet and Kazakhstan.

If we look at the two cases of ethnic conflict from a comparative perspetive, which is the purpose of this whole study, the following points will emerge.

First, almost all the demonstrations followed a particular pattern. Tibetans' recourse to express their anti-Chinese and nationelist sentiments has been religious symbolism. Everyday religious practices-especially 'circumambusation' served as a means of protest. Display of flags and circumambulation preceeded slogan-shouting at various demonstrartions. Throughout the course of the demonstration,even when provoked by the Chinese security personnel,Tibetans followed a strict discipline. They were unarmed and non-violent. Unlike Tibetans, Kazakhs followed a violent pattern. Demonstrators used home-made arms, iron bars, stones and inflamable mixtures unsparingly. Symbols hardly played any role during the demonstrations. But mosques and mausoleums were renovated after the riots. Sufi saints of pre-Soviet era have suddenly become 'natinal heroes'. For example, today Ahmed Yasava is regarded as Kazakh national saint.[134] More than religious, this kind of revival appears to be a gesture of re-assertion of Kazakh Muslim identity which is different from the Russian identity.

Second,the sites chosen for staging demonstration were of particular religious significance-Jokhang Temple and Ramoche temple, Ignoring party offices or more sinified ares of Tibet and sticking to the traditional old parts of Lhasa, demonstrates the assertion of their territorial integrity.Kazakhs, however, assembled infront of party offices—Central Committee and Executive Committee buildings—to show the strength of their nationalist and anti-Russian feelings.

Third, one more peculiar character of mass demonstrations in Tibet has been that these events were led by monks and nuns of the highest religious order including few trainee monks. Hence the demonstrations were mostly peaceful and non-violent. In Kazakhstan, religious leaders (mullahs) never appeared publicly during demonstrations. Members of Komsomol and young student leaders took the intiative in organizing anti-Russian protests. They were often joined by hooligans and other anti-social elements. Therefore, the demonstration were always violent involing frequent clashes between militia and the protesters. However, destruction of public (vehicles, police-stations, official buildings) and private (shops, private establishments) property is a common feature in Tibet as well as in Kazakhstan. Butt the degree of destruction (including loss of human lives) is greater in Tibet than in Kazakhstan.

Fourth, anti-Chinese and anti-Russian slogans were part of the demonstration in both the cases. In case of Tibetans, they underlined pro-independence feelings: Down with Chinese Repression' 'Independence for Tibet', 'Free Tibet'. Kazakh slogans valued 'autonomy' more than 'independence'. The demonstrators carried banners on which slogans were written in both Kazakh and Russian languages. These slogans included, 'Autonomy and separate seat for Kazakhstan,' 'Kolbin, Go back to Russia', America is with us, Russia against US' 'Kazakhstan for Kazakhs.'

Fifth, the nature of ethnic conflict in Tibet is mainly inter-ethnic *i.e.* between Tibetans and the Chinese. It was never intra-ethnic. On the other hand, ethnic conflict in Kazakhstan was both inter-ethnic and intra-ethnic. It was interethnic—between Russians and Kazakhs in Alma-Ata riots. At other places skirmishs occured among non Russian nationalities residing in Kazakhstan—Caucasians, Azerbanjans, Chechens etc.

Sixth, in case of Tibet conflict centered around political tensions—forcible occupation of Tibet Over the years, population transfer policies and other repressive measures aggravated socio-economic tensions. Where as in Kazakhstan latent socio-economic tensions were brought to the lime light after the change in political leadership- replacement of Kunayev (Kazakh) by Gennedy Kokbin (Russian). For example, presence of caucasians caused social injustice of Kazakhs in the Novy Uzen province and led to clashes between them.

Seventh, the demonstrations were more centred in Lhasa than in any other parts of Tibet. Besides, they did not have immediate repercussions either in neighbouring non-Chinese provinces or in other parts of Chinese territory. Contrary to this, events in Kazakhstan moved the whole country. A series of violent ethnic disturbances were reported by the press—Riga (late December 1986 and early January 1987), Demonstration by Jews in Moscow (February 1987), Armeica (February 1988) Ferghena valley in Uzbekistan (June 1988)... the list went on. So many demonstrations in so short a time were unprecedented in Soviet history. Finally the declarations of Sovereignty by the Baltic Republic (Lithuania, Latvia and Estonia) heralded the process of Soviet disunion.

Eighth, modernization and liberalization in Tibet and Kazakhstan, undoubtedly, raised the standards of living. When Kazakhs compare themselves with their Muslim brothers abroad they find themselves definitely in a better position. However, the status of Tibetans is less remarkable.This may be attributed to their conservatism. Tibtan in exile, on the other hand, seem to have progressed better. Upward mobility is negligible in the case of Tibetans, Kazakhs, managed to occupy posts at party and administrative levels. But in both the cases the key posts are monopolized by the Chinese and Russians respectively. Deng's four modernization process could not end separatist tendencies among Tibetans. Similarly, Gorbachev's efforts at Perestroika and Glasnost accelarated moves towards more autonomy or independence. The starting point was Alma-Ata in Kazakhstan, the most russified republic in Soviet Union's soft underbelly i.e. Central Asia. These unprecedented developments had ethnic connotations and surprised Gorbachev and his supporters of reform. Both Tibet and Kazakhstan experienced ethno national resurgence which politized ethnicity to a great extent.

Ninth, the struggle for independence, in the case of Tibetans, was on, right since the occupation of their territory by China. Exposure to western ideas further strengthened their ethnic identities and nationalist aspirations. Though Chinese initiated the process of dialogue with the dalai Lama in December 1978, both the parties have not found agreeable solutions and Tibetans continue to struggle for their long cherished goal—independence. Coming to Kazakhs, they did revolt for autonomous status before incorporation into the Soviet Union. The Bolshevik leaders appeased Muslim nations with promises of self-determination and right to session. Of late, they realized that these promises were hollow even after gaining republican status. Nationalist feelings were nurtured throughout the Soviet era but found expression under Gorbachev. Thanks to his reforms which brought nationalist sentiments into open. All said and done, Kazakhs never wanted complete independence because of their dependence on Moscow. They always aspired for more autonomy with true "self-determination" in issues related to them. Nazarbayev, president of Kazakhstan was the last supporter of Soviet disintegr ation and Kazakhstan declared independence later than other republics of Central Asia. Thus independence was thrut upon Kazakhstan and it joined Commonwealth of Independent States.

Resurgence of ethnic conflict has become a common phenomenon in all multicthnic states of the modern world. Between 1986 and 1991, the two comunist giants China and the former Soviet-Union witnessed a series of ethnic conflicts. This demonstrates the failure of Marxism to cope with ethnicity. In Tibet alone, 140 demonstratons took place from 1987 to 1992. In Kazakhstan demonstrations were not so frequent but disturbances spread to neighbouring republics in no time and led to system-wide breakdown of the Soviet empire.

These differences in outcome as well as in the modes of

struggle may be traced to different constitutional statues (regional autonomy or right to self-determination), cultural differences (Islamic or Buddhist derivatives) and different demographic imbalances.

Foot Notes:

1. John Bray, "China and Tibet an end to empire?" *World Today*, vol. 46, no. 12, December 1990, p.221.
2, *Tibet the Facts,* a report prepared by the Scientific Buddhist Association for the UNCHR, Tibetan Young Buddhist Association (Dharamshala, 1990), p.10.
3. Denison Ross, 'The Land of the Lamas and its Story' in J.A. Hammerton ed. *An Encyclopedia of Human Races All over the World,* Vol. 7 (Delhi, Gian Publishers, 1985) p. 4919.
4. T. Shakaba, *Tibet: A Political History,* (New York, Potala, 1984), p.25.
5. Georges Dreyfus, 'Cherished Memories, Cherished Communities', article (Spring 1993) Williamstown Mass.
6. Dawa Norbu, *Culture and the Politics of Third World Nationalism,* (London Routledge, 1992) p.69.
7. *Renmin Ribao*, (Beijing) April 4, 1988, pp. 1-3.
8. Dawa Norbu op.cit, n.6, p.208.
9. Heather Stoddard, 'Tibet from Budhism to Communism' *Government and oppositin*, 21 (1), WINTER 1986, p. 76.
10. Ronald D. Schwartz, *Circle of Protest,* (London, Hurst & Co., 1994), p. 221.
11. Ibid. p. 215.
12. Dawa Norbu, op. cit. no. 6, p.69.
13. 'Kazakhastan' Introductory Survey, *The Europa Year Book*, (London, Europa Publications Limited 1994,) p.1675
14. Martha Brill Olcott, 'Central Asia:The Reformers Challenge a Traditional Society' in Lubomyr Hajda and mark Bessinger, *The Nationalities Factor in Soviet Politics and Society*. (Boulder, Colorado, Westview Press, 1990), p.253.
15. Guy G.Imart, Kirghizhia-Kazakhstan: A Hinge or A Fault-Line, *Problems of Communism,* Sept-Oct 1990, p.1.
16. Rashid Ahmed, *The Resurgence of Central Asia:Islam or Nationalism* (London, Zed Books, 1994), p.1-9.
17. Katz ed., *Hand Book of Major Soviet Nationalities* (New York, Free Press, 1975), p.223.

18. *Summary of World Broadcasts,* (SWB)Part I USSR, 14 Fed, 1987.
19. *Current Digest of Soviet Press,* (CDSP), vol.39, no.19, April 1987, p.11.
20 *Kazakhstanya Pravda, June 10, 1989.*
21. Rasheeduddin Khan, 'Central Asia's Geo-political importance', *World Focus*, , Nov-Dec, 1992, p.59.
22. Rasma Karklins, *Ethnic Relations in USSR,* (London, Allen & Unwin, 1986), p.196.
23. Martha Brill, Olcott Op cit, n12, PP.269-270.
24 For example, the Kazakhs have embraced Ahmad Yasawi the first great Turkic Saint, mystic and builder of the Yasawi Sufi order. His tomb is in the town of Turkestan, He is considered as a Kazakh national saint, although the Kazakhs appeared on the historical scene several centuries after his death.
25. Ahmed Rashid, 'Bless Perestroika and send Korans', *Indpendent,_* 4, June 1990.
26. Ibid.
27. See Harold Bockman, The Brewing Ethnic Conflict in China', in Kumar Rupesinghe t.al. ed., Ethnicity and Conflict in a Post-Communist World (New York, St Martin Press, 1992), p.92.
28. Ronald D. Schwartz, op.cit, n.10, p.28.
29. Ibid p.92.
30. Samten G. Karmay, 'Identity: Language Ritual and Culture', in Robert Barnett and Shirin Akiner, *Resistance and Reform in Tibet* (London Hurst, & Co, 1994), 0p.114.
31. Tsering W. Shakya, 'Politicization and Tibetan Language', in, Ibid., p.164.
32. Herbert Adams Gibbons, *Nationalism and Internationalism* (New York 1930), p.4.
33. The name dates back to 1917. Alash Orda Kazakh National Party Organized Third All Kazakh National Congress in Orenburg. It proclaimed the autonomy of the Kazakh-Kyrghiz region and set up the Provisional People's Council of Alash-Orda.
34. Marie Broxup, 'Islam in Central Asia since Gorbachev' *Asian Affairs* (London), vol.18, Part 3, October 1987, pp. 283-293.
35. Martha Brill Olcott, op.cit, n.14, p.274.
36. Ibid p. 274.

37. Saidbaev, *Islam i obshchestvo*. 1978) p. 191, quoted in Martha Bill Olcott, op, . cit, n. 14, p. 271.
38. Hall, Stuart, 'The Question of Cultural Identity' in *Modernity and its Futures*, (Oxford, U.K. Blackwell, 1990), p.312..
39. James G. Kellas, *The Politics of Nationalism and Ethnicity*, (London Macmillan, 1991), p.29.
40. Dawa Norbu, op.cit, n.6, p. 225.
41. Ibid, p.84.
42. Ibid, p.109.
43. Ronald D. Schwartz, *Circle of Protest,* (London Hurst and Company, 1994), p.20.
44. Asha Hans, 'Tibetan Ethnicity and the Chinese Policy', in K. Warikoo and Dawa Norbu (ed.), *Ethnicity and Politics in Central Asia* (New Delhi, South Asia Publishers, 1992, p.178.
45. *The Observer* (London), Sunday, 4 October 1987.
46. Lhasa Xizang Regional Service in Mandarian, 24 September, 1987, in *Foreign Broadcast Information Service,* 1 October 1987: 27.
47. *Tibet the Facts,* op.cit, n.26, p.84.
48. *1987 Uprising in Tibet,* (Dharmasala, Assembly of Tibetan People's Deputies, 1988), p.1.
49. *Indian Express,* Thursday, October 1, 1987.
50. Ibid.
51. *1987 Uprising in Tibet,* Eye Witness Account, pp.35-6.
52. the Guardian. (London), October 3, 1987.
53. Schwartz, op.cit, n.43, p.25.
54. *Tibet the Facts,* op.cit, n.26, p.86.
55. *The Washington Post,* Thursday October 8, 1987.
56. Schwartz. op.cit, n.43, p.26.
57. Ibid, pp.28-29.
58. Ibid., p.33.
59. Lhasa Xizang Regional Service in Mandarin, 1130 hrs GMT, October 13, 1987 in *FBIS* February 10, 1988, p.30.
60. For details see Martin King Whyte, *Small Groups and Political Rituals in China* (Berkeley, University of California Press, 1974).
61. Beijin Xinhua in English, 2 October 1987, in *FBIS,* 5 October, 1987: 26.
62. Lhasa Xizang Regional Service in Mandarin, 9 February 1988, *in*

FBIS, 10 February, 1988: 38.

63. Beijing, *Xinhua,* in English, 21 January 1988 in *FBIS* 21 January 1988:33.
64. First demonstration by nums occurred on 19 December. At another demonstration students put up posters demanding Tibetan independence, use of Tibetan language at school, an end to forced sterilization and improved facilities. Monks also joined them.
65. Tsepon W.Shakabpa, *Tibet :A Political History,* (New York, Potala Publications: 1984), pp. 6,85.
66. *Tibetan Bulletin,* 'Monks Boycott Great Prayer Festival', vol.19, no.1, Jan-April 1988, p.8.
67. Lhasa Xizang Regional Service in Mandarin, 23 February, 1988, in *FBIS* 24 February 1988: 25.
68. Trering Dhondup. 'A First Hand Account of the March Riot in Lhasa', *Tibetan Review,* My 1988, p.6-7 Schwartz, op.cit, pp.77-83. For more official and western interpretations and witness accounts see Donnet, pp. 121-5.
69. *The Observer,* and May, 1988, 'Tibet': Murder in the Temple', by Jonathan Mirsty and *Bulletin* issued b. Lhasang Tering, President of the Tibetan Youth Congress, 'Tibet's Holiest Temple Turned into Death Trap', Press Rekease, 4 May, 1988.
70. *The Observer,* op.cit.
71. Dhondup, op.cit., n.69.
72. *Tibetan Review,* 144 Monks, Missing since March Riot', p.4.
73. *Tibet the Facts,* op.cit, n.26, pp.93-94.
74. *Bureau of His Holiness: The Dalai Lama,* (Delhi), Press Release, Jue, 3, 1988.
75. See Schwartz, op.cit, n.43, p. 97-98.
76. For further information refer Hanna Havnevik, *Tibetan Budhist Nuns,* (Oslo; Universitetsforlaget, 1990), p.84.
77. *Tibetan Review,* July, 1988, p.4.
78. Tibetan Bulletin. Vol. 19, no. 1, Jan-April 1988. p. 27 and Tibet the Facts. op. cit. p. 97.
79. Tibetan Review. July 1988, More Demonstrations Depite Heavy Clampdown, p.4.
80. Tibetan Revie, October, 1988, p.4
81. *Guardian* September, 14, 1988, 'Tibetian Police Crackdown on

Rebel Monks, by Jasper Baker, *Amnesty International,* Newsletter, PRC 'Public Trial Monks New Crackdown in Tibet' October 1988, vol.18, no.10.

82. It is a it page document preparet by Drepung monks in the summer of 1988 titled: The meaning of the Previous Democratic of Tibet.
83. Schwartz, op.cit, n.43, p.128.
84. Ibid., p.137-8.
85. Ibid., p.141.
86. Beijing, *Xinhua,* in English, 11 December, 1988, in *FBIS,* 12 December 1988:44.
87. *The Guardian,* 'Tibetan on Rights Marcn Peking', December 19, 1988.
88. Beijing Xinhua in English January 29, in *FBIS*; January 30, 1989:67.
89. Schwartz, op.cit, n.43, p.152.
90. Lhasa Tibet-Regional Service in Mandarin, January, 31, 1989, in *FBIS*_February 1, 1989: 18.
91. Schwartz op.cit, n.43, p.154.
92. Ibid., p.154-155.
93. Robert Delfs, 'Repression Repeated' *Far Eastern Economic Review,* March, 16, 1989, p.10-11.
94. For move details see *Amnesty International,* Urgent Action PRC. Fear of Mass Arrests/Tourture/Summary Executions, March 8, 1989.
95. *The Observer,* 'The Secret "Massacre" by Jonathan Mirstky, August 12, 1990.
96. Beijing, *Xinhua* in english, 21 March 1989, in *FBIS,* MARCH 22, 1989:23.
97. Few Tibetans after release from prison denied this and said. They did not intend mark the day in any manner.
98. Se Appendix in Robert Mc Corquodale and Nicholes Orosz ed, *Tibet, The Position in International Law*, (London Edition Hansjorg Mayer, 1994), p. 219.
99. Ahmed Rashid, *The Resurgence of Central Asia Islam or Nationalism,* (London; Zed books, 1994), p.47.
100. 'The Events in Kazakhastan: An Eyewitness report', From Akriv Samizdata, AC 5913 (10 April, 1987), *Central Asian Survey,* vol. 6, n.3, p. 73.

102. Ibid.
103. Martha Brill Olcott, 'Perestroika in Kazakhstan', *Problems of Communism,* July-Aug, 1990, p.66.
104. Eyewitness Account: op.cit, n.100,p.73-74.
105. Tass December 18,1986, *SWB* part I USSR, Jan 1, 1987 and *Daily Review* (Moscow) Novosti Press Agency, Vol.33, no.8155.
106. *SWB*, Part I, USSR, I Jan, 1987.
107. Kazakhastanskaya Pravda, 10 June,1989.
108. Eyewitness Account, op.cit, n.100, pp.74-75.
109. Ibid.
110. SWB part I USSR, 1 Jun. 1987.
111. Martha Brill Olcott, "Perestroika in Kazakhstan *Problems of Communism*, July—Aug. 1990, p.67.
112. Current Digest of Soviet Press (CDSP), vol. XLII no. 39, Oct.31, 1990 p.22.
113. Ibid. p.23.
114. Amir Taheri *Crescent in a Red Sky*, (London Hutchinson London; 1989), p.192.
115. *New York Times,* 11 January, 1987.
116. *CDSP,* vol.37, no.51, January, 1987, pp.1-2 *SWB* Part I, USSR, SU, 84461, 19 December, 1986.
117. *TASS*, 21 January, 1987.
118. A one dayf conference on internationalist education took place in Alma-Ata in April, 1987.
119. *SWB,* Part I USSR, SU/8451/i, 29, December, 1987.
120. Tass Report in English, 21 January 1987, in *FBIS,* Daily Report, 28 January 1987, p.28, Pravda, 26 June 1981, *FBIS* Daily Report 26 June 1987, p. R.5 and 19 February 1968, p.49.
121. Bess Brown, 'The Public Role in Perestroika', *Central Asian Survey*, vol.4, no.3, 1990, pp.87-96.
122. Ibid.
123. CDSP, Vol. XLI, no.25, 1989, p.19.
124. Ibid, p.20.
125. Ibid.
126. Ibid., p.21
127. Ibid,
128. Yaccov Roi, 'Islam and Nationalism in Soviet Central Asia',

Problems of Communism (Washington) July-August, 1990, p.55.

129. CDSP, vol. XLI, no.25, 1989, p.20.

130. Ibid, p.21.

131. *SWB,* Part I USSR, May 2 1989.

132. Kuzio, no.101, p.100.

133. Kuzio,op.cit,no.101,pp.99-100.

134. Maria Eva Subteleny, 'The cult of holy Places, Religion Practices among Soviet Muslims', *The Middle-East Joural* Autumn, 1989, pp. 593-604.

6

Constitutional Statuses of Tibet and Kazakhstan

The Soviet Union and, to a least extent, China gave their minority nationalities impressive concessions within the framework of Marxist-Leninist principles. These concessions aimed at socio-economic transformation of these nationalities on socialist lines in practice, generated strong feelings of nationalism. This chapter will examine the constitutional statuses of Tibet and Kazakhstan since their incorporation into Communist regimes. While Tibet was forcibly brought under Chinese rule by the PLA. Kazakhs were gradually drawn into the Soviet orbit with the division of Turkestan,[1] on ethnic lines, by the Bols hevik leadership. It will also be examined how various official policies and programmes led to demographic imbalance and distorted representation of nationalities in major power structures of their de jure territories.

Tibet

Much before the formation of Peoples Republic of China, Chinese claimed that Tibetans were one of the five races of China, Symbolically, they were supposed to have been represented by the five horizontal bars Hans, Manchus, Tibetan, Mongols and the Tatars. This reflected the relative prominence of these ethnic groups among the rest of fifty-one other national minorities. As early as at the Second Congress of the CCP in 1922, the manifesto of the Congress proposed that China proper, including Manchuria (the present Northeast), was to bee a true democratic republic and that the three regions of Mongolia, Tibet and Turkestan (present day Xinjiag) were to be autonomous, forming self-governing regions. China, Mongolia, Tibet and Turkestan would then unite on the basis of their own free will thereby establishing a Chinese federal republic.[2] Again, in November 1931, CCP adopted a Draft Constitution of the First-All-China Congress of Soviets and also passed a lengthy resolution on the 'nationality question' in China it proclaimed that all are equal before the Soviet law and shall be citizens of Soviet Republic without any distinctions[3] The proclamations were modelled after the 1924 Soviet Constitution. The 1931 constitution recognized the right to self-determination of the national minorities in China, their right to complete separation from China and to the formation of an independent state for each national minority.[4]

In 1949, People's Liberation Army became victorious with the defeat of Kuomintang forces and on October 1 Mao announced the formation of 'people's Republic of China'(PRC). At that time there was no mention of the idea of federalism self-determination or the right to secede. These ideas underwent a dramatic change. They were sinified gradually to suit 'Chinese characteristics'. The original (first) Constitution of China (1954) declared China to be a 'single multi-national state' of which the 'national autonomous areas are inalienable parts' (Articles 3).[5] The later documents of the constitutions (1975,1978 and 1982) followed the same tone.

In the same year, *i.e.*, 1949 divisions of the People's Liberation Army crossed into Tibet at eight points of the Tibetan border. By the end of October 1950, the small Tibetan army, consisting of 8,000 men, was defeated and the provincial capital of Chamdo had been captured.[6] After this event, Tibet was compelled to sign Seventeen Point Agreement prepared by the Chinese. This agreement aimed to incorporate Tibet into China while only granting 'regional autonomy' in return. However, China agreed not to alter the existing political system in Tibet and not to interfere with the established status, functions and powers of the Dalai Lama or the Panchen Lama. Along with regional autonomy, China further agreed to respect the religious beliefs and customs of Tibetans. These promises were hardly put into practice and Chinese continue to maintain their suzerinity over Tibet on the basis of the Seventeen-Point Agreement till today.[7]

According to Chinese, Tibet is only that area under the actual authority of the Dalai Lama's government in 1950. Later, this part became Tibetan Autonomous Region (TAR) Other Tibetan areas were made into autonomous districts in the neighbouring Chinese provinces-Yunnan, Sichuan, Gansu and Qinghai. Thus, more than half of the Tibetan territory and population was excluded from the TAR. After attaining the status of Autonomous Region in 1965, Tibet was to have more freedom is regard to local matters. The law Governing Regional National Autonomy stipulated "People's Congress in the areas of national autonomy of specific regulations in accordance with the political, economic and cultural characteristics of the local nationalities.[8] However, the autonomy was greatly circumscribed as Tibetans have to do everything through the guidance and approval of the Central Government. This was made clear as early as in 1952. According to the General Program of the PRC for the Implementation of Regional Autonomy for minorities (1952), "the autonomous organ of each autonomous area is a local government led by the government of the next higher level, under the unified leadership of the central government". (Article 2) The local government can draw up…special regulations for the region...but these shall be submitted for approval to the People's Government of the two next higher levels (Article 23)[9].

Both the Chinese and the Tibetan officials in Tibet have only the power to endorse and implement the policy directives issued from Beijing. This process of governing is justified on the basis of 'democratic centralism. Thus, autonomy of the region meant no more than a limited delegation of authority from the central government in Beijing to the local authorities in Lhasa. The Chinese presence is felt throughout Tibet. Virtually all positions of power are occupied by the Chinese military and Community Party officials and only few prominent Tibetans[10] have been appointed to positions of nominal importance. Various political and administrative rights are subordinated to national programs, laws and regulations. Besides this, local security forces are totally under the control of the "unified military system of the state"[11] In other words, Tibetan were denied democratic rights in their own territory despite autonomous status since 1965.

Demographic Situation

Chinese policies of assimilation and integration distorted the demographic balance of this region as a whole. The very demarcation of western and central Tibet as 'Tibet' and exclusion of traditional areas inhabited by Tibetans from 'Tibetan' territory was the first step by Chinese in this regard. The implementation of population transfer policies right from 1950s has become the easiest means to reduce Tibetans to an insignificant minority. This was done and still continuing in the name of development, maintenance of law and order in Tibet by the Chinese 'elder brothers'. Population estimates by officials or individuals have been highly inaccurate. However, their single point of agreement was that the population of Tibet has been declining. Today, Tibetans in exile and their supporters routinely use the figure of six million for the entire worldwide population of ethnic Tibetans. The Chinese say that the total Tibetan population is only slightly more than four million. However, the official Chinese statistics themselves reveal that it was over six million in 1959. According to the China's State Statistical Bureau, the TAR had 1,273,969 people in November 1959. Tibetan areas of Kham (then known as Sikang by China) had 3,381,064 Tibetans. In Qinghai and other Tibetan areas incorporated into Gansu. Tibetan were reported to number 1,675,534. The total these three figures stands at 6,330,567[12]. When the first national census was conducted in 18953, Tibet had one million people as reported to the census organizations by the then local government of Tibet. The results of the fourth national census in July 1990, show that Tibetan population is 2,196,000 of whom 2,096,000 are Tibetans. The population of Tibet increased by more than one time between the period of 1953 and 1990.[13] (see Table I)

Generally, the official population statistics published by PRC refer only to TAR. This area comprises more than half of the total area traditionally claimed by Tibetans to constitute Tibet or 'historic' Tibet. According to this claim, Tibet proper included the north eastern province of Amdo and the eastern province of Kham. It was stated in Chinese White Paper that in 1953 besides 1 million Tibetan inside Tibet, there were 1.77 million residing outside Tibet. Two comments may be made here: (1) at all times the PRC has apparently had no difficulty in identifying and counting Tibetans as a separate and distinct people; and (2) the fact that in 1953 the number of Tibetan living outside TAR was so much greater than those living in TAR (a ratio of almost 2:1) is evidence consistent with although not conclusive of the fact that the area of Tibet extended beyond the borders of TAR.[14]

The Chinese contend against this fact and blame the imbalance to the decline of Tibetan Population before their takeover.[16] The reasons put forward by the Chinese are not congruent with the growing Chinese population.

TABLE I

Chinese Official Estimates of Population in Tibet*

Year	Tibetans	#	Han	#	Other Ethnic Groups	#	Total
1964	1,209,000	96.63	37,000	3	5,000	0.37	1,251,000
1982	1,786,500	94.4	91,700	4.85	14,000	0.75	1,892,200
1990	2,096,000	95.46	81,200	3.75	18,400	0.84	2,195,600

According to the Tibetan sources, the estimates included for all the areas inhabited by Tibetans—'Historic 'Tibet. These figures put the number of Chinese at 7.5 million as against the 6.0 millions Tibetan in Tibet. The distribution is as follows.[15]

TABLE II

Region	Tibetans	Chinese
Central Tibet (TAR)	1.9	over 2
Amdo (Renamed Qinghai)	0.8	2.5
Kham (Incorporated into Szechuan, Yunnan, Gansu)	3.3	3.0

After Hu Yaobang's visit to Tibet in 1980, a reform package was to be launched in Tibet. Withdrawing Han cadres considerably was one of its main points. In the early 1980s few older cadres were withdrawn, but their numbers were rapidly supplanted by a new influx of technical and administrative workers, entrepreneurs, and labourers—partly resulting from government policies and partly a function of the new economic freedoms made possible by the reforms. In the eyes of Tibetans, this influx has continued unabated from the mid 1980s to the present, perceptibly increasing after the suppression of protest in 1989. Most of these 'outsiders' became permanent settlers. This idea was formulated by Mao as early as in 1952, in the "Directive on Central Committee of CCP on the Policies of work in Tibet". He proposed a fivefold increase in the TAR population. To quote his words, "Tibet covers a large area but is thinly populated. Its population should be increased from the present two or three million to five or six million, and then over to ten million.[17] In a statement to Legal Enquiry Committee of International Commission on Jurists on 29 August 1959, the Dalai Lama said: In 1955 just before returning to Lhasa we had been to see Liu-shao-chi. He mentioned to the Panchen Lama that Tibet was big country and unoccupied and that China had a big population which can be settled there. Another statement by Premier Zhou Enlai said: The Chinese are greater in number and more developed in economy and culture but in the region they inhabit, there is not much arable land left and underground resources are not as abundant as in the regions inhabited by paternal nationalities.

This kind of attitude had serious impact on ethnic relations between Tibetans and Chinese. The continuous flow of Chinese immigrants into Tibet promises to negate the cause of Tibetan self-determination thus rendering all internal resistance as something negligible. If the present rate of Chinese migration is continued, it will reduce the efforts of the Dalai Lama and exile to unrealistic claims by turn of the century. Within a short period, by the turn of this century, however, a point of no return may well be crossed in Tibet itself. The infrastructure that China is currently building will then be ready for a truly massive migration to commence far surprising Mao's 1952 projection of 10 million Chinese in Tibet. Beijing portrays its intention solely beneficent claiming its migrants are's killed labour' sent to develop Tibet for Tibetans, and then leave when the job is done. Contrary to this claim, the settlers instead of being 'engineers' and 'contractors' as they are termed, are young., poorly educated and encouraged to intermarry and settle down in small business or farming. They are mainly drawn by the prevalent unemployment in China Proper.[18.]

TABLE III
Ethnic-Trends in the Kazakh SSR
(in thousands)

	1959	1970	1979	1989	Percentage Change 1959-89	Percentage Change 1989
Kazakhs	2,795	4,234	5,289	6,535	+133.8	39.7
Russians	3,974	5,522	5,991	6,228	+56.7	37.8
Ukrainians	762	934	898	896	+17.6	5.4
Germans	660	858	900	958	+45.2	5.8
Tatars	192	288	313[b]	328[b]	+70.8	2.0
Uzbeks	137	216	263	332	+142.3	2.0
Belorussians	107	198	181	183	+71.0	1.1
Uighurs	60	121	148	185	+208.3	1.1
Koreans	74	82	92	103	+39.2	0.3
Azerbaijani	36	58	73	90	+136.8	0.5
Poles	53	61.4	61.1	60	+13.2	0.4
Bashkirs	9	21	32	42	+366.7	0.3
Moldovans	15	26	30	33	+120.0	0.2
Mordva	25	34	31	30	+20.0	0.2
Dungans	10	17	22	30	+200.0	0.2
Chuvash	11	23	22	22	+100.0	0.1
Jews	23	28	22.8[a]	18.5	-33.9	0.1
Others	345	288	337	391	+13.3	2.4
Total	9,295	13,009	14,684	16,464	+77.1	100.0

a The 1989 census adjusted the number of Jews listed in the 1979 count from 23,466 to 22,762.

b The figures for 1979 and 1989 do not include the Crimean Tatas, who were counted as Tataras in previous censuses. The 1979 census listed a Tatar population of 313,160 in the Kazakh SSR. The 1989 census listed the 1979 Tatar Population of Kazakhstan as 312,626. The difference of 834 was listed in the 1989 census as the Crimean Tatar population of Kazakhstan in 1979; the 1989 Crimean Tatar population of Kazakhstan was isted as 3.169.

Source: Lee Schwartz, USSR Nationality Distribution by Republic, *soviet Geography,* vol. 32, no. 4, 1991, p. 238.

The sharp increase since the last decade is as follows. In May 1984 Radio Beijing reported that: "Over 60,000 workers, representing the veneered groups in help in the construction work in the TAR are arriving in Tibet daily (number of days not mentioned) and have started their preliminary work. They will be helping in the electricity department, schools, hotels, cultural institutions and construction of mills and factories.[19] Another 60,000 Chinese workers mainly from Sichuan arrived in the "TAR" in the summer of 1985.[20] In 1991, announced that "technicians from all over China have come to work at various construction sites and about 3,00,000 workers are prepared to join in the project.[21]

In Lhasa alone, there were 50,000 to 60,000 ordinary Chinese residents in 1985. From 1985 to 1988 additional Chinese immigrants doubled the population of Lhasa. That this development created problems for the Tibetan population was recognized by the "TAR" Government. In March 1989, Ngapo Ngawang Jigme Vice-President of the Chinese National People's Congress said that "today because of so many Chinese shopkeepers and settlers coming into Tibet (some 1,00,000 of them being in Lhasa alone) great disturbance has been caused to public security.[22] This phenomenon also incites some social and ethnic problems.

The concentration of Chinese in Kham and Amdo seems to be at its highest. This process started even before 1959. This colonization of the region by Han Chinese was an attempt to wipeout Tibetan ethnic character.[23] As in TAR they were supposed to 'help' Tibetans. Many builders, workers and technicians came in flocks to 'develop' Tibet. Tibetans considered them a drain on their economy and interpreted the policy as an insidious attempt to complete the sinization of their country. According to the late Panchen Lama:

The expense of keeping one Chinese in Tibet is equal to

that of four in China. Why should Tibet send its money to feed them...Tibet has suffered greatly because of the policy of sending a large number of useless people. The Chinese population in Tibet started with a few thousands and today it has multiplied manifold.[24]

To encourage Chinese settlement in Tibet Chinese Government offered various incentives. Housing, hospitals, cinemas and schools and specials food items are made available to lure Chinese. Higher wages and extra allowances are paid. Long vacations are allowed. For Chinese enterprises, special tax exemptions and law-interest loans have become major attractions. Tibetans are denied incenses to start new enterprises in their own land, Economic open-door policy in late 1992 further accentuated settlement of Chinese population in Tibet. New Chinese launchings and villages are emerging in many parts of the TAR such as Droma (Yatung), Emagang, Phenpo, Tsethang, Toelung, Nyemo, Kongpo Nyingtri and Maldro Gyama.[25] To add to all these, coercive birth control measures are being imposed to control population growth of Tibetans.[26]

Many Chinese officials and technical experts who have been sent to Tibet created a Chinese layer of administration and technical expertise along Tibetan society. As a result, Tibetan are relegated to a secondary position in all spheres of life. Almost all key administrative positions are grabbed by the Chinese. The policies of liberalization put emphasis on training of Tibetan cadres. As Jigme Ngapo points out, the Tibetan autonomy advocated by Hu Yaobang remained a dead letter. Though Tibetans cadres have been upgraded they do menial jobs while Han cadres give directives. The right to "veto" central government policy is only ornamental. Except tax exemptions other measures suggested by Hu had no substance.

China claims to have launched democratic reform in Tibet. New Political system of people's democracy has made Tibetans masters of the country. This assertion is beyond truth. Though the TAR is 'autonomous'. Tibetans have little or no say in running their own affairs. Chinese have final say in all the matters. Regional Party's First Secretary has always been a Chinese. He was later followed by Zhang Guohua, Zeng Yongya, Ren Rong Yi Fatang.Wu Jinghua, Hu Jintao and Chen Kuiyuan (1992 on wards).[27] Even the highest Tibetan officials, like Ngapo Ngawang Jigme, have no power to make decisions on their own. They need to consent their Chinese subordinates. They were asked to stay outside Tibet and pay occasional visits as and when required by the Chinese Government. For example, Chinese restricted the movement of the late Panchen Lama.

Tibetan representatives have no freedom to express their views at various political meetings. The pre-determined proposals and their approval are always glorified as 'democratic' decisions of the Tibetan people. The arrangement of Chinese hierarchy in Tibet is such that right from the highest to the lowest official is assisted by a Junior Chinese subordinate who exercises the 'real' power. In most important offices such as the so-called TAR Economic Planning Department and the Personnel Department, Chinese officials and clerical staff always far out number Tibetans.

Elections are always held in an undemocratic manner. Pre-determined list of candidates becomes the final list of victorious candidates in the elections. Inspite of all these manipulations Tibetan in TAR are definitely in a better 'position compared to their brothers in the neighbouring provinces. In Khan Amdo regions Tibetans are deprived of their political identity and they are being reduced to an insignificant minority of electorates in their own land.[28]

The general economic impact of Chinese settlers on Tibetans has been disastrous. The most fertile lands, the best jobs, regions with most modern facilities are occupied by the Chinese. Almost 30,000 workers in Lhasa's 16 labour units were replaced by

Chinese in 1985 alone. The increasing presence of Chinese population has created a major challenge to Tibetan livelihoods.[29] Sinocization of Tibet has been taking place in the guise of economic reforms which, in effect, resulted in massive Chinese exodus to Tibet. This in turn led to scarcity of resources, rationing to Tibetans, segregation. Paradoxically, these very processes (including opening Tibet to tourists) nurtured nationalistic feelings among Tibetans. The concepts of democracy, human rights, self-determination, 'real autonomy' are better understood by Tibetans at a time when repression of Tibetans genuine aspirations is at its peak.

Anti-Chinese and pro-independence demonstrations inside Tibet have not created any ripplies either in the neighbouring provinces or by other ethnic groups in any part of China. Except for Xinjiang, and Tiananmen square event, other areas are not under ethnic turmoil. The centralization of nationalist demonstrations in Lhasa has not led to countrywide crisis. With the genuine support of voluntary organizations, (especially from the west) and world-wide campaigns the issue of Tibet has received great attention by countries of the world. Many parliaments passed resolutions for restoration of human rights in Tibet. Tibetan's faith in Buddhist principles worked worders. It kept their nationalist spirit alive even after four and a half decades of communist rule.

Kazakhstan

During the Revolution of 1917, Lenin and the Bolsheviks used the slogan of the right to self-determination as a tremendously effective political weapon in winning the non-Russian regions to their side. Ethno-nationalism became the basis on which socialist federalism was constructed. A socialist federated state was considered to be composed of ethno-political administrative units, in which each indigenous socialist nation had its own 'state hood'—as opposed to 'bourgeoi federalism' where the constituent parts were held to be primarily economic-regional formations. All Soviet Constituent, Union and Republican, embodied the 'principle of a right to self-determination for ethnonations, up to and including the right secession. In a way the federal structure of the USSR has had the significant effect of strengthening.

On 20 November 1917, the Russian Bolshevik government, the Council of People's Commissioners addressed an appeal signed by Lenin and Stalin, specifically to the Moslems:

> From today, your beliefs and customs and your national and cultural institutions are declared free and inviolate. You are entitled to this—Know that your rights, like the rights of all peoples of Russia, are protected by the whole might of the Revolution and its agencies, the Soviet of Workers', Soldiers and Peasants' Deputies, Support then, this Revolution and its Sovereign Government.

This Proclamation did not console the non-Russian Muslim nationalities. In December 1917, Alash-Orda, provincial people's council has formed by Kazakhs. It proclaimed the autonomy of the Kazakh-Kirghiz regions. Similar regional councils were set up in other parts of central Asia Despite this, by 1920, Lenin regarded the Soviet republics as already linked in a de-facto federation. Soviet power was further consolidated with the granting of republican or autonomous status within the Soviet Federation. In Central Asia, Turkestan Soviet Socialist Republic was created in 1921.

During the initial natinal-delimination of territories on ethnic lines in 1924. Turkestan was divided into autonomous units. Kazakhs areas fell under Kara-Kyrghaz autonomous province. The first USSR Constitution came into existence in the same year. Kazakh Autonomous province was created in 1925. The ongoing social reform led to further modification of republican constitution. A new constitution was adopted in 1936. Under the constitution republics would enjoy autonomous status. Each republic has its own Party organization, council of ministers, Supreme Soviet, Constitution, flag hymn and capital city. At this juncture, Kazakhs were elevated to the republican status, with its capital in Alma-Ata.[30] This kind of sovereignty is largely symbolic while dependence on Moscow is very real.

The latest Constitution (1977) set for the constitutional bases for republican rights priority in chapters 8 through 19 (Articles 70-150). In many respects if followed the 1936 Constitution. It describes USSR as 'union of Sovereign states (Article 76). Some important provisions are:residuary power rest with the Union (Article 80), authority to co-ordinate and control the activities of production and administrative organization located on republic's territory, was granted to the union republic (Article 77). However, there are few exceptions, Under Article 75 right to secession is abridged. The article noted: the territory of the Union of Soviet Socialist Republics is a single entity and comprises the territories of the union republics. In addition to this, right to have own military formation (which was never exercised by the republics before) was not re-affirmed. The unifying influence of Communist Party in politics and society figured prominently. In other words, real power is vested in the unitary Communist Party, representative of class (i.e. proletarian-internationalist) interests. The party's monopoly of political power in legitimated by Marxist-Leninist ideology. State has become mere executive arm of the party.

Both party and state hierarchies are run along vertical control lines from the top downward, according to an operational principle of 'democratic centralism' which was designed to reduce any national, regional or local input to a mere formality.[31] Lenin's policy created an image of 'voluntary federation in reality, it is neither voluntary nor a federation. Instead, it instituted a centralized unitary state that carried the seeds of its own destruction, because it gave the component nations and nationalities the forms but not the substance, of national existence and political power.[32]

Demographic Situation

The ethnic composition of the population of Kazakhstan has changed remarkable over the years. If the years preceeding Soviet era, Central Asia and Kazakhstan served as a dumping ground for political deportees and industrial labour. Kazakhs were forced to settle on land contrary to their nomadic life styles. Under Soviet rule parts of Kazakhstan were heavily industrialized, while communication and infrastructure greatly improved. However, Kazakhstan was one of the worst affected regions during the campaign in the early 1930s to collectivize agriculture and settle nomadic peoples. More than one million people are estimated to have died as a result of starvation and famine. While Russian population nearly doubled from 1.3. million in 1917 to 2.5 million by 1939 during the same period Kazakhs sustained an absolute population decline from 3.7 million to 2.3. million. [33] Second world war brought another wave of deportees, including German, Crimean Taters, Cancasians from different parts of the USSR.[34] The Kazakh holocaust exceeded that of any other nation in the Soviet Union at that time. Again, in the early 1960s Khrushehev's Virgin Lands Scheme brought into Northern Kazakhastan, the lost larger group of one a half million European settlers.[35] Thus, Kazakhstan became international gradually. This phenomenon caused some resentment among the native Kazahs. Kazakh national consciousness that arose in response to the flood of Russians was both anti-Russian and Anti-Czarist.

Broadly speaking Kazakas today is ethnically bifurcated

state with the Russians and Ukrainian dominating the Northern and Eastern Regions and indigenous Kazakhs tending to predominate in the western and southern parts. The capital city of Alma-Ata located in the South provides an exception as Russians are in majority here comprising about fifty per cent of its population even today. In 1979 Kazakhs represented only 36 per cent of the total population where as non-Kazakhs were in majority (Russians—40.8 per cent, Ukrainians—6.1 per cent and Germans—6 per cent and others 11.1 per cent).[36] In the census count of 1989, the Kazakhs constituted a majority (39.7 per cent) in their own republic for the first time since the early years of the Union. The Russian population declined from 42.7 per cent in 1959 to 37.8 per cent in 1989. (See Table III). By the year 2000 A.D. it is likely to be reduced to 30 per cent. In view of the low birth rates of Russians and decline in the migration from European parts of the USSR into the Kazakh Republic and continued high Kazakh fertility, some Kazakh news papers have even forecast an increase in the population of Kazakhs to 50 per cent in 2000 A.D. and a further rise upto 65 to 70 percent[37] For more clear picture of demographic trends (see Table IV),

In the late 1980s, after the launching of Perestroika and glasnost, demographic Russification tended to nationlize Kazakhs and orient massbased nationlism against both Russian immigrants and Moscow, in a greater degree than before. These developments were utilized by Kazakh nationlists to mobilize Kazakh population behind a separalist political action programme.[38] A Russian sense of Kazakh favouritism and feeling of relative deprivation have increased since 1989, along with the adoptation of new laws.

(1) Language law that proclaimed Kazakh as the official language of the state, and (2) citizenship law that allowed Kazakhs

Table IV. Russian and Kazakh Population by Oblast, 1959-1993 (percentage)

Oblast	Russians					Kazakhs				
	1959	1970	1979	1989	1993	1959	1970	1979	1989	1993
South										
Aktubinsk	26.2	26.4	25.1	23.7	22.0	43.1	47.5	52.1	55.5	59.8
Almaty (Oblast)[a]	42.4	37.8	35.3	31.2	29.4	32.1	38.3	31.3	45.3	50.2
Gur'yev[b]	20.7	27.3	27.0	22.8	19.8	72.2	62.4	63.1	67.3	71.2
Zhambyl	31.4	32.4	30.4	26.5	24.1	39.1	40.7	44.0	48.8	56.7
Kzyl-Orda	15.3	18.6	15.3	13.3	11.6	72.2	69.9	76.2	79.4	83.9
Chimkent[c]	22.7	22.0	19.2	15.3	13.7	44.1	47.2	51.0	55.7	59.4
Almaty (capital)	73.0	70.3	66.0	59.1	56.0	8.6	12.1	16.4	22.5	25.1
North										
East Kazakhstan	70.0	69.5	67.7	65.9	64.2	18.9	23.2	25.4	27.3	29.1
Kokshetau	41.7	40.4	40.4	42.1	39.5	18.5	22.8	26.3	28.9	31.6
Pavlodar	39.3	44.4	45.9	45.4	44.6	25.5	25.2	26.8	28.6	30.9
North Kazakhstan	64.5	63.5	63.4	62.1	61.7	12.5	14.9	16.6	18.7	19.5
Semipalatinsk	45.2	40.9	39.1	36.0	34.5	35.8	43.7	48.0	51.9	55.6
Ural'sk[d]	41.5	38.4	37.2	34.4	33.3	45.9	49.3	51.5	55.8	57.6
Akmola + Karaganda + Kustanay + Turgay + Zhezkazgan[e]	44.2	47.3	47.5	45.7	45.7	18.8	18.7	21.1	23.7	26.0

a. Figures for Ahnaty Oblast include Taldy-Kurgan Oblast, which was part of Almaty in 1959.

b. Figures for Gur'yev Oblast (renamed Atyrau in 1992) include Mangistau Oblast, which was part of Gur'yev in 1959, 1970, and 1989.

c. Chimkent Oblast was renamed South Kazakhstan in 1992.

d. Ural'sk Oblast was renamed West Kazakhstan in 1992.

e. In order to create a geographically comparable unit, it was necessary to combine figures for these oblasts. Zhezkazgan was part of Karaganda in 1959 and 1970, Turgay was part of Kustanay and Akmola (Tschnograd until 1992) in 1959 and 1989, and territory was reallocated from Akmola Oblast to Karaganda Oblast in 1993.

Source. 1959. BSU SSSR, *1962*, pp. 112-172, 1970. BSU SSSR, 1973. pp. 232-252, *1979* Goskomsat SSSR, 1989, pp. 188-277, *1789* Goskomstat 1991, pp. 22-116, *1993* Goskomstat RK, 1593. pp. 47-48.

living outside Kazakhstan to be citizens of the state but refused to allow dual citizenship for Russians. (3) Constitution that proclaimed independence in the name of Kazakh nation. As a result, Russian emigration (especially from the southern parts of Kazakhstan where Russians are minority) to Russia began and it is likely to continue: a 1994 public opinion poll found that approximately one-third of all Russian wished to leave Kazakhstan. The finding held true for Russin-dominmated northern oblasts of Kazakhstan. On the other hand, in 1992-93,43,000 Kazakhs arrived from Mongolia, 20,000 from Russia, and 25,000 from Uzbekistan and other Central Asian States.[39] The settlement of this new wave of Kazakhs in Russian dominated Kazakhstan is perceived by Russians as a deliberate effort by the Kazakh government to Kazakhize" the population in the north.[40] Despite these facts, Russian populatin in Kazakhstan has not decreased significantly. Russian concerntrartion in the north reflects geographic variations in phasing-in of the law on languages. This law already has been implemented in Kazakh majority southern oblasts, but has been delayed in Kazakh-majority northern oblasts.[41] The presence of Russians is also felt in the composition of power-structure in Kazakhstan. In 1920s, party membership campaigns brought many young Kazakhs into its fold. This had a dramatic impact. In 1924 only 8 per cent of the party members were Kazakh compared to 40 per cent in the mid-1960s. In this later period the population of Kazakhastan who were party members exceeded the proportion of Kazakhs (about 33 per cent) in the total population of Kazakhstan.[42] Likewise, Kazakhs were over represented in the Kazakh Supreme Soviet comprising about 40 per cent of the delegate, and among leading party officials. A study of Kazakh party leaders in the 1955-65 period showed that apoproximately half of all provincial, district and city first secretaries were ethnically Kazakh.[43] However, Russians played more prominent role in the administration of

Kazakhstan than in other Central Asian republics since 1950s. The decision to turn northern Kazakhstan into a major grain producing area meant that Moscow had to have reliable cadres in place. Thus from 1954 throgh 1959 Khrushchev dispatched a series of senior Russian officials, most of them with extensive background in agriculture as first and second secretaries of Kazakhstan's Communist Party, including Leonid Brezhnev, who served in Kazakhstan in 1954-56 . This practice was a deviation from the general estblished rule in late Stalin years: first secretiries came from the indigenous nationality and second secretaries, generally charged with few direct ties to the areas of their assignment. Only in 1960 was a Kazakh again appointed either of these positions. This was a protege of Brezhnev—Dinmukhamed Kunayev. Russians also staffed virtually all key posts—heads of principal economic ministries, deputies in these ministries headed by locals.[44]

With the accession the Brezhnev, the party elites of the Kazakh nationality came to dominate the political life of Kazakhstan. Kunayev was reappointed first secretary in December 1964. Kunayev, promoted to the politburo in 1971, a rate privilege for Central Asian leaders, established republic wide party network that eventually encompassed both Russian and Kazakh. While the pattern of appointing Russians as second secretaries persisted, by the mid-1970s these men were more Kunayev's creatures than Moscow's[45] Brezhnev era was a period of remarkable political stability throughout Central Asian Region. Though few Central Asian occupied very few posts in the CPSU Central Committee membership, the majority of these came from Central Asia.

After Brezhnev's death, events took a different turn. A severe campaign to weed out corrupt and inefficient leaders was initiated by Andropov and it gained momentum during Gorbachev era. Negative phenomenon in Kazakhstan—nepotism, corruption, low levels of growth in various sectors, inefficiency in administration was highly publicized, Kunayev's position was undermined with the dismissal of his loyalists. At the Twenty-seventh party congress of the CPSU these issues were discussed at some length. New secretaries were appointed in all the republics of Central Asia. The consequences of this step in Kazakhstan were unexpected. The forces that it unleashed continue to have implications for nationality politics before and after the disintegration of the Soviet Union. The announcement of Kunayev's retirement and his replacement by an ethnic Russian paved the way for unprecedented nationlist demonstrations in the Soviet Union.

The starting point was Alma-Ata. Kolbin served the republic for three years. Many changes occurred in party life. Multi candidate elections for the leadership of Communist Youth League began in 1988.

In March 1989, Nursultan Nazerbayev replaced Kolbin as First Secretary. He has been a supporter of Gorbachev's reforms. At the same time he attempted to fulfil the kazakh nationlist desire for greater socio-cultural, economic and political Kazakhization while reassuring the Russians that their state would be protected. However, this formula proved unworkable, since increasingly Kazakh privileges necessarily restructured the national stratification system to the detriment of Russians. Russians are nurturing a feeling of deprivation in the administration Russian dominated areas of Kazakhstan. To add to these feelings Kazakh political elites are against any concessions to Russians in an independent Kazakhstan since December 1991.

Many local political appointees throughout the country were replaced by Nazerbayev's own personnel.[46] The recent parliamentary elections.[47] (See Appendix IV) in Kazakhstan provide further evidence of political Kazakhization of the state, and its effect on the functioning of a 'democratic, legally regulated state'.[48] There were 754 registered candidates in the parliamentary elections. Out of them, 566 were ethnic Kazakhs and 103 Russians. 70,000 German were represented by seven candidates and the 2,00,000 Uighurs by four voters turnout was 75 per cent one of the observers remarked: "The purpose of elections in pluralist free societies, that of being afforded an opportunity to determine their true war not achieved." There were also complaints about same person voting several times, complex system of registration of candidates, less propaganda about election manifestoes and improper count and destruction of surplus ballots.[49] These allegations were denied by the Chairman of Central Electoral Commission of kazakhstan. Final Results say that out of 176 deputies of Supreme Kenges (The new name of Supreme Soviet) about 90 per cent represent nomenklatura, that is, heads of various state institutions and local administration, directors of industrial enterprises and collective farms. This is based on the official report of the Central Electoral Commission, published in Kazakhstankaia Pravda, 17 March 1994.[50] The 176 deputies included 22 women representation. The ethnic composition is as follows: 105 Kazakhs; 49 Russian; 10 Ukrainians; 3 Germans; 3 Jews; once Uzbek; one Tatar; one Korean; one Pole and One Uighur. Among these 42 were from state list, 75 nominated and 59 self-nominated candidates. According to an independent group of analysts 60 per cent of the elected were reliable supporters of Nazarbayev[51] Though Kazakhs constituted about 42 per cent of the population, they became an obvious electoral majority. They nominated 77 per cent of the candidates. This caused fear about actual unrepresentation of non-Kazakhs in the power structure. These results further exacerbated relations between Russians and Kazakhstan. Some Russians demand annexation of northern territories to Russia.

A detailed analysis of the demographic trends and party power structure reveals that Kazakhstan never wanted total

Table V Russians and Kazakhs in Kazakhstan, 1959-1993
(absolute number and percentage of total population)

Nation	1959	1970	1979	1989	1993
Russians	3,974,229	5,521,917	5,991,205	6,227,549	6,168,740
Percentage	42.7	42.4	40.5	37.8	36.5
Kazakhs	2,794,966	4,234,166	5,289,349	6,534,616	7,296,942
Percentage	30.0	32.5	36.0	39.7	43.1

Source: 1959 TsSu SSSR, 1962; 1970: TsSu SSSR. 1973, p. 223; 1979: Goskomstat SSSR, 1989. p. 179; 1989 Goskomstat KSSR, 1991, p.23; 1991: Goskomstat RK.. 1993, p.45.

Table VI *National Composition of the Kazakh and Central Asian Republic Party Organizations*

	1954		1950		1955		1960		1965		1970	
	No.	%	No.	%	No.	%	No.	%	No.	%	No.	%
Kazakh organization												
Kazakhs	49255	43.1	91600	40.6	93363	39.9	115357	36.2	148755	33.0	190892	34.3
Russians	39685	34.7	91656	40.6	97028	41.4	138147	43.4	201918	44.8	242991	43.7
Central Asians	53176	46.5	99821	44.3	101905	43.5	126163	39.6	164393	36.5	201671	37.9
Europeans	51563	45.1	115304	51.1	123022	52.5	176769	55.0	259621	57.6	310202	55.7
Others	9522	8.3	10431	4.6	9161	3.9	15570	4.9	26472	5.9	35715	6.4
Total	114261	100.0	225556	100.0	234193	100.0	318502	100.0	450486	100.0	556508	100.0

independence from the Soviet Union. In fact it was one of the last republics to declare sovereignty. When independence was thrust upon Kazakhstan, she was left with inter-ethnic tensions. Russian emigration, unemployment, low productivity and a myriad of problems. Though Kazakhstan has rich mineral resources which are yet to be tapped, political situation inside the state will decide future prospects. Kazakhstan gained international recognition as soon as it became independent. She has signed treaties on economic co-operation, cultural exchange with many developed and developing countries including China, U.S. and India. Time and again Nazarbayev emphasized the importance of having cordial relations with Russia for economic and political reasons. The presence of Russian majority in northern parts of Kazakhstan is a sensitive issue to cope with.

Despite various problems, Kazakhstan seems relatively stable and peaceful compared to her neighbouring Muslim Asian republics.

Nazarbayev has to act more tactfully in dealing with national relations in order to maintain political stability and territorial integrity of the nation.

Comparative Analysis

A thorough understanding of the constitutional statuses to Tibet and Kazakhstan, recent demographic trends and representation of minorities in the power structure further tells us that the conscientious policies towards minority nationalities. (Tibetans and Kazakhs among others) have been unsuccessful in achieving their goal—assimilation and integration into their respecting dominant nations. It we look at the past history of Tibet i.e., pre 1950 period, there exists evidences which justify that Tibet enjoyed all rights as an independent nation. It had diplomatic relations with neighbouring countries Nepal, Bhutan, India and signed treaties. In the post - 1950 period. i.e., after the forcible signing of the Seventeen-Point Agreement and invasion by the PLA, Tibet lost her power as a nation. Mao and his successors never considered minority groups as 'nations'. This may be attributed to the proportion of minorities in Chinese population as a whole. Minorities constituted a mere 8 per cent of the population and Tibetans constitute less then 1 per cent among them. The remaining 92 per cent are Han Chinese. On the other hand, Kazakhstan did not have any characteristics of a nation before 1917. Kazakhs were nomands in the steppe region. During 16th century Kazakhs converted to Islam. Religion gave them a sense of belonging to a community, moral character and regulated their life-styles to a great extent. After the revolutions minorities in the periphery areas or borderlands were incorporated into the Soviet Federation. National delimitation on ethnic lines gave them territorial integrity while republican status bestowed upon them nationhood. Considering the proportion of minority nationalities in the USSR which is nearly 50 per cent, (Kazakhs represent 2.1 per cent as per 1989 census) Lenin and the successive leaders continued to put up with these nations' which were on par with Russia as constituent republics of the Soviet Federation to maintain *Status quo* Unlike China, Soviet Union had more diverse ethnic populations. While Chinese rule destroyed historical and cultural identity of Tibetans Soviet rule strengthened ethnic cohesiveness of Kazakhs.

Mao followed Soviet steps in dealing with minorities for a brief period of time. Later, he found "national-regional autonomy" as an alternative to self-determination to suit Chinese environment which has more homogeneous population. The concept of 'regional autonomy' was further narrowed after People's Republic of China came into existence. After the Dalai Lama's departure in 1959, china declared the dissolution of the government of Tibet. A few years later, in 1965, when Tibetan Autonomous region was formed excluding traditional Tibetan-inhabited areas of Kham and Amdo, new power structures replaced the old ones. Kashag,

National Assembly, monk council etc. were replaced by Party Police, work Teams etc. Thus the religious socio-cultural life of Tibetans was forced to change drastically under Chinese rule. Since Kazakhstan became union republic with a right to 'self-determination' extended upto a right to secession, a new set of political and administrative apparatuses, similar to their presence felt- Constitution, flag, Communist Party Militia Academy of Social Sciences, to mention a few. These concessions given to Soviet minorities may be seen as a desperate attempt to contain separates identities. Despite the fact the Tibet an autonomous region and Kazakhstan was Union republic, in practice, they enjoyed little or no autonomy and self-determination in dealing with their own problems. In both the cases, central or state law always prevailed over regional or national laws.

The representation of minorities in major power structures and decision-making bodies varies in both cases under study. But they exercised no 'real' powers and always were under the supervision of Chinese or Russians as the case may be. At the regional level Tibetans did represent at power structures. But at the central level they are unrepresented. Kazakhs enjoy a better position in this regard. They always occupied, with few exceptions, number one posts at the regional level and they are represented in equal proportion to their population. After independence, the first democratic elections were held in March 1994 in Kazakhstan. The non-Kazakhs, especially, Russians are unhappy about the over-representation of Kazakhs in the Parliament-Supreme Kenges. In Tibet and Kazakhstan (before independence), however, the key posts are dominated by the majority Chinese or Russians.

If one examines the demographic trends in Tibet and kazakhstan, two different courses may be noted. The population transfer politics are still operational in Tibet. Besides, Chinese follow a nation-wide population policy which is more strictly implemented in TAR and other areas inhabited by Tibetans.[52] Forced abortions and sterilisations are further attempts to reduce and eliminate Tibetan population in their homeland.[53] Today, Tibetans find themselves marginalised in economic, political educational and social spheres. In Kazakhstan, contrary to the case of Tibetans, demographic trends favoured Kazakh population. The high fertility rates of Kazakhs with low fertility rates among Russians resulted in dramatic change. For the first time since 1917 they became majority in their own republic in 989. In Soviet Union there were no attempts to control population. Besides Kazakh Muslims are against following any such measure, since they violate the sacred principles of Islamic religion. After the independence, though Russians are leaving Kazakhstan, their number has not reduced significantly and they are still a majority in many northern regions and Alma-Ata in the South. Population transfer policies aimed at reducing Tibetans and Kazakhs into minorities in their own territories, however, created resentment in both the cases.

Deng and Gorbachev wanted to reform economic stagnation without deviating from Communist or Socialist principles. Four modernization processes in China and Perestroika and Glasnost in Russia besides giving more freedoms to minority populations to re-structure their economic lives (and also political life in the Soviet Union) strengthened ethnic separatism. This was unintended and unexpected by the Chinese as well as Soviet leadership. In China the process of liberalization was more controlled and the resurgence of ethnic nationalism is restricted to few minority areas, especially TAR. In the Soviet Union liberalization had far-reaching effects. It led to revival of non-Russian nationalism and demands, for independence everywhere ultimately, this system-wide crises led to disintegration of the Soviet Union itself.

Except for international awareness in recent years. Tibetans did not receive any powerful support to achieve their goal. While dealing with the Tibetan cause at national parliaments many nations have passed resolutions condemning violation of basic human rights of Tibetans by China. At the international forums, they are less vocal and over-poqered by national interests. China's dialogue with the Dalai Lama (started in 1979 came to an abrupt end. Further negotiation have not resumed so far, though the Dalai Lama is ready to accept limited independence. If pro-democracy movement succeeds in China there is hope for higher degree of autonomy and semi-independence to Tibet in near future. Unlike Tibet Kazakhastan became independent for different reasons. In Soviet Union, there were country-wide ethno-national movements. Besides, the neigh-bouring Islamic nations whole—heartedly supported independent moves by Kazakhstan and other Central Asian Republics. Kazakhastan always aspired for 'real autonomy' and true self-determination. Though Kazakhstan never wanted total independence, the interplay of political and socio-economic forces forced her to be independent and ... find solutions to old and new problems that threaten the stability and integrity of the nation. Compared to her neighbouring Asian republics, without doubt, Kazakhastan is experiencing relative calm and stability within the region.

These are the main reasons which led to different outcomes: independence in the case of Kazakhstan and *status quo* in the case of Tibet, despite several similarities in the two cases as we have noted throughout this study.

Foot Notes:

1. Central Asia was known as 'Turkestan' under Russian rule. It was annexed to Russia in 1880.
2. Conrad Brandt, Benjamin Schwartz and John K.Fairbank, *A Documentary History of Chinese Communism*, (London, Allen & Unwin, 1952), P.64.
3. Ibid, p.221.
4. For more details see ibid, pp.220-224.
5. *The Constitution of the People's Republic of China* (Peking, Foreign Language Press, 1954).
6. See Kashag Document 11 (4)3; Military Communique on Entry of Chinese Army into Tibet, New China news Agency (Beijing), 8 November1950; zhang Guohuna, "Tibetan Returns to the Bosom of the Motherland", Renmin Ribao (*People's Daily)*, 25 October 1962.
7. This agreement was never acceptable to Tibetans since the Tibetan negotiators were not allowed to consult their government, Threats of an immediate occupation of Lhasa left them with little choice.
8. 'Tibet-Its Ownership and Human Rights Situation' Informaton Office of the State Council of the People's Republic of China',September 1992, Beijing, *Beijing Review,*September 28-October4, 1992,p.28.
9. Cited in Harrold Hinton,'The Status of National Minorities in Com-munist China,USIA,IRI, *Intelligence Survey* (15-63-55), July 1955, pp.7,9, National Archives, Diplomatic Branch, Washington,D.C.
10 For example, Ngapoi Nagwang Jigme became minister in Tibetan local government in 1950. In 1965 he became chairman of the People's Committee of the Tibet Autonomous Region.
11. Article 53, The Common Program of the Chinese People's Political Consultative Conference and Article 70, Constitution of the People's Republic of China.
12. *People's Daily,* Beijing,10 November 1959.
13. 38-43 paras of the PRC Reply to UNHRRC 48th Session E/CN/ 4/1992/37) 5 January 1992 and China's White Paper on Tibet (FE/1494 CI)Beijing, China 24 September 1992. These figures

exlcluded non-TAR regions with Tibetans.

* Compiled from different sources

14. Peter Grogan, The Relevcant Territory of Tibet Population Transfer in Appendix B of Robert McCorquofdale and Nicholas Orosz ed, *Tibet:The Position in International Law*, (London, Edition Hansforg Mayer and Seridia, 1994).
15. *The 1987 Uprising in Tibet*, Assembly of Tibetan People's deputies Dharmasala p.187. for more details see, Michael C, van Walt van Praag, Population Taransfer and the survival of Tibetan Identity' *Strategic Dogest* vol.18, no.1 pp.35-50.
16. Jan Anderson, "Tibetan: A Dwindling Population-A Comparative Study" *Tibetan Review,*vol.16, no.1, October 1981,pp.6-13.
17. Remin Ribao, 22 November, 1952, *FBIS*23 November,1952.
18. Mc.Corquodale and Qrosz, op.cit., n.14, p.187.
19. Radio Beijing 14 May 1984.
20. *China's Population,* (Beijing,1988)
21. *Beijing Review,* 21-27 January 1991.
22. Beijing *Renmin Ribao*in Chinese, 23 March 1989,p.2. in FBIS,24 March 1989, p.21.
23. Jayaprapkash Narayan,Presidential Address at Afro-Asian Convention on Tibet and AGainst Colonialism is Asia and Africa, 9 April 1969, New Delhi, p.6.
24. Cited in Anand Kumar ed., Tibet:A Source Book,(New Delhi Radiank Publishers,1995), P.90.
25. iBID.,P.91.
26. For more information see, *Tibetan Review:Study Confirm Population Transfer,*(New Delhi:October 1995) and R.Schwartz, *circle of protest* (1995\4), PP.203-205.
27. See Appendix I.
28. Anand Kumar, op.cit, n.23, p.82.
29. W.P.Ledger, *The Chinese and Human Rights in Tibet,* p.18,J.F.Awdon, *Tibet Today,* (Special) Report Series, The U.S.Committee, New York,1987), p.13.
30. For a detailed account of formation of republics see, Ahmed Rashid (1994), *The resurgence of Central Asia*, Bohdar Mahdyo and Victor Swoboda (1989), *Soviet Disunion,*, Richard pipes (1954), *The formation of Soviet Union.*

31. Teresa Rakoska Harmstone,'Chicken coming home to Roost: A perspective on Soviet (ethnic relations Journal of *International Affairs* vol.25 No. 2 winter 1992 p.522.
32. Ibid.
33. See Robert Kaiser and Jef chinn; Russian-Kazakhastan' *Post-Soviet Geography,* 36(5), p.258.
34. 'Kazakhastan: Intyoductory Survey' *The Europa World Year Book,* (London, Europa Publication, 1994)p.1675.
35. Milan Hanuer 'Geo-politics in the last 100 years', *Central Asian Survey,* (London), vol. 8, no.1, 1989.
36. K.Warikoo, 'Soviet Central Asia in Ferment' in Warikoo and Dawa Norbu eds. *Ethnicity and Politics in Central Asia,* (New Delhi, South Asia, Publishers, 1992), p.64.
37. Richard Weeks, *Muslim Peoples,* (London, Greenwood Press 1975),p.210.
38. Martha olcott,'Perestroyka in Kazakhastan', *Problem of Communism,*
39. (4),p.69.
40. CDSP op.cit, n.37,'
41. Martha Olcott, 'Kazakhstan:A Republic of Minorities' in Ian Bremmer and' Ray Taras ed. *Nation and politics in the Soviet Successor States,* (Cambridge, Cambridge Univercity Press, 1993), p. 320.
42. Katz,H.B.of Major Muslim Soviet N (New York.,Free Press, 1975), p.221.
43. Ibid.
44. for details on post-Stalin period in Kazakhstan See Martha Brill Olcott. The Kazakhs, (Stanford, CA, Hoover Institution Press, 1987) chap.10.
45. There was, in any case, no real potential for a conflict of interests between Moscow and Kazakhstanduring these years, as Brezhenv had de facto ceded a great deal of control over affairs in the republic to Kunayv.
46. Olcott op cit n. 40, p. 326.
47. Election were held on 7 March 1994 with 123 foreign observers from 24 countries to monitor the elections.
48. Nazerbyev's promise in November 1994, before December 1991

elections in which he won majority of the votes.

49. *Summary of World Broad Casts,* partl, 3,9,16 March, 1994.
50. Kirill Nourzhenov and Amin Saikal. 'The new kazakhstan; has something gone wrong?' *World today* n.12, December 1994, p.226.
51. *Summary of World Broadcasts,* Part 1, 19 March 1994, for Party wise distribution of seats see ibid, 16 March 1994.
52. According to census estimates, China's minority population is growing at a faster rate than the Han population: Minorities increased from 5.8 per cent of the total population in 1964 to 8 peered cent in 1987 see *China Daily,* June, 22, 1990.
53. For details see Anand Kuar, op.cit., n.23, pp.91-97.

CONCLUSION

Numerous studies of ethnicity have appeared in recent years, making it one of the most widely studied political phenomenan of modern times. In the present context an attempt is made to analyse ethnic conflict in Central Asia from a comparative perspective. The two cases under study—Tibet and Kazakhstan have special significance. Among Chinese minorities Tibetans' struggle for independence, the intensity of their pro-independence feelings,are not only greater than other minority nationalities but are exceptional. Their deep faith in the Dalai Lama and Buddhism have been motivating factors.

Kazakhstan is the only republic of former Soviet Union with titular nationalities in minority. Inspite of increasing Russian presence under Soviet rule and greater industrialization and development levels, proportional representation in power structure, the first ethnic disturbances in Gorbachev era occurred in its capital, Alma-Ata. The events triggered a chain reaction throughout the former Soviet Union. Since major ethnic demonstration occurred around the same time (in an era of liberalization and democratization) in Tibet and Kazakhstan, the two cases are ideal for a comparative analysis. During the course of this study the following hypotheses are tested.

First, ethnic conflict in Central Asia is facilitated by the over all liberalization policies in the Soviet and Chinese societies. Communist reforms led to the emergence of civil societies and simultaneously strengthened ethnic ties. The negative results of liberalization—population transfer, economic crisis, scarcity of resources, loosening of controls with regard to religion and culture accentuated ethno-national feeling and realization of absence of true democratic rights. All these phenomena led to conflict of interests among the ethnic groups involved—Tibetans vs Chinese, Kazakhs vs Russians.

Second, ethnic conflict is co-rrelated to worsening economic conditions in the two societies. In case of Tibet, though industrialization took place to improve the economic conditions, the fruits of this process are hardly enjoyed by native Tibetans. Domination of Chinese in key posts of economic life resulted in unemployment, and poor living standards of Tibetans when compared to migrated Chinese who are given all the facilities including more incentives and allowances. This attempt has been a means to under populate Tibetans and make their presence insignificant in their homeland.

In Kazakhstan, Gorbachev launched Perestroika to restructure economic life to end stagnation and other negative phenomenon-low productivity etc. This process started with purges in Republican Party leadership which was supposed to facilitate new set of reforms. The replacement of Kunayev by an ethnic Russian, Kolbin led to violent ethnic clashes.

Third, the moving spirit of ethnic conflict is the assertion of ethnic identities manifested in language, culture, religion etc. Tibetans used various forms of religious practices as a means of protest at various demonstrations. Language and cultural symbols also played an important role in expressing nationalist feelings. Kazakhs, though most Russified among Central Asians, used religious, cultural symbols, historic figures to assert their ethnic identity. Similarly many new journals appeared in Kazakhs language to portray only Kazakh people. Thus Tibetans and Kazakhs strongly felt that their ethnic identities were distinctly opposite to the Chinese and the Russians respectively.

Fourth, the use of religion, culture, language for expressing nationalsit feelings further reveals the tenacity of these factors as political weapons. This clearly shows that politicization of ethnicity is taking place in Tibet and Kazakhstan in an unprecedented manner.

Fifth despite some similarities between ethnic conflict in Tibet and Kazakhstan, they led to different outcomes. This may be explained in the light of legitimation crisis faced by the state (unitary and federal frame works) international factor (recognition but no support in case of Tibet, and both recognition and support from the Islamic for kazakhstan States), the population size of the minority in question. The last point-population size, played a crucial role in assessing the result of ethnic conflict in Central Asia. In China, minorities constitute a mere 8 per cent whereas in Soviet Union they constituted nearly half of the total population. Chinese adopted an Unitary farmework which gave not more than autonomy to its minorities. Since the former Soviet Union gave republican status to Kazakhstan on par with Russia it enjoys in theory, right to selfdetermination upto a right to secession. Thus the federal framework with constitutional right made independence moves easier in Soviet Union than in China. In other words. In Soviet Union the structure of legitimacy of nationhood was legally recognized. Paradoxically, nationalism which is the concomitant manifestation of such nationhood, was squarely denied. Herein lies the central contradiction out of which post-Communist nationalism arose as the inevitable,public expression of nationhood.

When hegemonic controls were loosening with the advent of Perestroika and Glasnost, anti-Russian and nationalist sentiments were expressed publicly by non-Russian minorities. Thus, when conditions were ripe, ethnic nationalism could unite all segments of the population against Moscow and evenly supply leadership in the form of existing republican institutions and elites, established by the Soviet Constitution itself and legitimated by decades of propaganda. Similar conditions are absent with regard to Tibet. However, it may be hoped that the growing nationalist aspirations may be realized if pro-democracy movement succeeds in China. In a speech delivered at the first Congress of Chinese students scholars in the United States, held in Chicago July 1989, Yan Jiaqi proposed "federalism" (lianbang guojia) under a democratic system as the best hope both for reforming China's internal politics and ultimately for resolving the problems of Hongkong, Taiwan and Tibet.

A system-wide crisis in the Soviet Union led to forced independence of Kazakhstan along with other republics. In China the rigidity of the unitary system and the rule of PLA restricted the scope of independence for Tibetans. Despite this, Tibetans are prepared to sacrifice anything for reaching their goal of independence—including their lives and become martyrs. This reminds one of verses in Bhagavadgita (3:35 & 18:47) "Better is one's own law (Dharma) though in itself faulty than an alien law (Chinese rule) well accomplished. Surely death in one's law of being is better; perilous it is to follow the law of another's being'... "When one does work regulated by self-nature one doesn't incur sin". The Tibetan independence movement with its basis on peace and non-violence is remarkable. Change of moods is as natural to human beings as nations. The future of Tibet lies in the hope that a more honest and respectful relationship may one day emerge between Tibetans and the Chinese to fulfil the genuine nationalist aspirations of Tibetans within Tibet and in-exile. Kazakhstan too is hoping for a more friendly relations with Russia to cope with continuing and newly emerging problems after disintegration. In both the cases, the neighbouring nations have a positive role to play in brining about a peaceful change for a better tomorrow.

The emerging new Central Asia in the post-Communist era is a goldmine of issues and questions that concern policy makers, scholars and students of international relations.

APPENDIX - 1

PROVINCIAL-LEVEL LEADERS IN TIBETAN AREAS SINCE 1950

(pre-1979 names are given in Wade-Giles transliteration)

Tibet Autonomous Region: Party Leaders

November 1951 - August 1965. Zhang Jingwu (Chang ching-wu). First Secretary of the Tibet Work Committee of the CCP.

November 1960 - September 1965. Tan Guansan (T'an Kuan-san). May have been acting First Party Secretary or a high ranking Deputy Secretary. First Political Commissar of the Tibet Military Region, February 1952 to July 1967.

September 1965 - September 1967. Zhang Guohua (Chang Kuo-hus). Party Secretary of the TAR. Commander of the Tibet Military Region, October 1951 to September 1967. Acting Party Secretary on the Tibet Work Committee in early 1956. Deputy Chairman of the Preparatory Committee for the Autonomous Region of Tibet (PCART) from its inauguration in 1956 until its disbanding in September 1965. Party

Secretary, Sichuan, August 1971-1973.

*September 1968- August 1971.*Zeng Yongya (Tseng Yung-ya). Chairman of the Tibet Revolutionary Committee. Commander of the Tibet Military Region from February 1964 until January 1968.

August 1971-May 1980. Ren Rong (Jen Jung).TAR Party, Secretary and Chairman of the Tibet Revolutionary Committee. Political Commissar of the Tibet Military Region and Vice-Chairman of the TAR Revolutionary Committee from 1968. Deputy Political Commissar of the Tibet Military Region and of the Tibet Military District from September 1963 (the region was reduced to the Tibet Military District from September 1963 (the region was reduced to the status of a Military District in 1971). Held the rank of Major General from 1955.

May 1980-1985. Yin Fatang. Political Commissar of the Tibet Military District and Party Secretary of the TAR. With a PLA unit in Tibet 1950-67.

1985-July 1988. Wu Jinghua (Yi nationality). Party Secretary of the TAR. Returned to Beijing because of 'ill health': reportedly sacked for 'right deviationism'.

December 1988-1992. Hu Jintao.Party Secretary of the TAR. October 1990: returned to Beijing because of 'ill health'. October 1992: promoted to the standing Committee of the Politburo of the PCC.

December 1992-? Chen Kuiyuan. Party Secretary of the TAR. Vice Governor of the Inner Mongolian Autonomous Region in 1991. Member of the Party Committee of the Inner Mongolian Autonomous Region, responsible for higher education, from 1989.

Apparent Acting Party Leaders during Hu Jintao's Absence

March 1989. Zhang Shaosong. Political Commissar during martial law *(March 1989—May 1990);* apparently the effective leader of the TAR party Committee to July 1990.

July 1991. Raidi (Tibetan: Rakti) Described as Executive Deputy Party Secretary in July 1991;subsequently described as Deputy Part Secretary but listed before others until *March 1992* (see Chen Kuiyuan).

August 1991 - 1992. Zhang Xuezhong. Apparently leading Deputy Party Secretary, listed before Raidi and before the Governor of the TAR,Gyaltsen Norbu.

TAR Heads of the Government

1951 -9. Dalai Lama (Ta-lai-ma). Head of Local Government, *April 1951 to April 1956,* Chairman of the Preparatory Committee for the TAR (PCART),April 1956 to March 1959.

1959-64. Panchen Lama(Banqen Erdeni/Pan-ch'an E-erh Te-ni). Acting Director of the PCART,March 1959 to December 1964. Deputy Director, *May 1959 to March 1959*

March 1965 - September 1967. Ngapo Nagawang Jigme (A-p'ei A-wang Chin-me). Acting Director of the PCART, March 1959 to September 1965. First Chairman of the TAR from its foundation in September 1965 to September 1967. Deputy Chairman of PCART,March 1959 to March 1965. First Deputy Commander of the Tibet Military Region, September 1945 to March 1959. Deputy Commander, March 1959 to June 1964.

September 1968-August 1971. Zeng Yongya (Tseng Yung-ya). Chairman of the Tibet Revolutionary Committee. Commander of the Tibet Military Region,February 1964 *until January 1968.*

June 1971 - August 1979, Ren Rong (Jen Jung).Chairman of the Revolutionary Committee Party Secretary.

September 1979 -February 1981, Tian Bao (T'ien Pao)alias Sangye Yeshe. Chairman of the TAR,Vice-Governor of xikang (Sikang), November 1959 to January 1953. Vice-Governor of Sichuan, December 1955 to May 1967. Vice-Chairman of the Tibet Revolutionary Committee, 1968 to 1969. Deputy Party Secretary of the TAR, August 1971 to August 1978.Deputy Political Commissar of the Tibet Military Region, May 1970 to June 1971, Second Political Commissar of the Tibet Military District, 1973 to February 1981. Deputy Party Secretary in Sichuan, 1981-2.

April 1981 - August 1982. Ngapo Ngawang Jigme. Second term as Chairman of the TAR. Remained Chairman of the TAR People's Congress; later became a Vice-Chairman of the Standing Committee of the National People's Congress. Was First Deputy Commander of the Tibet Military District in 1979.

April 1983-1985, Dorje Tseten, Chairman of the TAR. Deputy Party Secretary, March 1983 to June 1985. Director of the China Institute of Tibetology. Beijing from 1985 to June 1985, Vice-Chairman of the TAR People's Congress for six months in 1981.

1985 - April 1990, Dorje Tsering, Chairman of the TAR.

May 1990-? Gyaltsen Norbu, Chairman of the TAR;Deputy Party Secretary.

Qinghai:Party Leaders

October 1949 - August 1954. Zhang Shoungliang (Chang Chonglinag). Party Secretary of Qinghai and Governor of Qinghai, November 1952 to December 1954.

August 1954 - October 1961. Gao feng (Kao Feng). Party Secretary of Qinghai.

November 1961 May 1962. Wang Zhao (Wang Zhao). Acting

First Party Secretary of the Qinghai Party Committee. Governor of Qinghai, q963; Deputy Political Commissar of the qinghai Military Region, 1965 to August 1967.

May 1962 - October 1966. Yang Zhilin (Yang Chih-lin). Party Secretary in Qinghai, first Political Commissar of the Qinghai Military Region, July 1964 to July 1965. Previously Governor of Suiyuan (since disbanded),late 1949; demoted to Vice-Governor of Suiyuan, December 1949 to December 1952. deputy Party Secretary of Inner Mongolia, July 1952 to May 1962.

March 1971 - September 1976. Liu Xianquan (Liu Hsien-Chu'uan), Party Secretary of Qinghai; Chairman of the Qinghai Revolutionary Committee.

August 1967 to March 1974. Commander of the PLA in Qinghai, December 1964 - February 1968. Commander of the Inner Mongolia Military Region for three months in 1967. Deputy Commander of the Lanzhou Military Region for nine months in 1968.

March 1977 - January 1980. Tan Qilong (T'an Ch'lung),party Secretary of Qinghai. First political commissar of the Qinghai Military District, March 1977 - September 1978. deputy Party Secretary of Zhejiang from 1949; first Party Secretary and Governor of Zhejiang, 1952-4,Governor of Shandong, 1954-5 and 1958-63, party Secretary of Shandong, 1961-7, Deputy Chairman of the Revolutionary Committee in fujian, 1970-2. Chairman of the Revolutionary Committee of Zhejiang, 1972-7.

January 1980 - January 1983. Liang Buting, Party Secretary. First Political Commissar of the Qinghai Military District, February 1980 - May 198. April 1983 - July 1**985.** Zhao Haifeng, Party Secretary, Qinghai, Vice-Governor of Qinghai in October 1981, First Political.

APPENDIX - 2

Chronolgy of Events in Kazakhstan

60-1200 AD Some Turkic tribes united by legendary figure Alaska Khan in southern Siberia, forerunner of Kazakh people.

1200 - 1500 Kazakh tribes migrate southward from Siberia.

1218 Central Asia devestated by Mongols hordes under Genghis Khan

1500 - 1600 Kazakh chiefs resist Uzbek confederacy. Founding of the three Ordas Kazakhs convert to Islam.

1731 -42 Kazakh ordas submit to Russian protection.

1757 Qirot tribes, who devastated Kazakhs, defeated by Chinese.

1783 -1870 Kazakhs lose 1 million people in anti-Russian revolts, famine and migration.

1822-48 Kazakh territory incorporated into Russia.

1853 Russians capture Kazakh seat of resistance at Kzyl-Orda.

1854 Vierny, later Alma-Ata, is founded by the Russians.

1860 Sino-Russian Treaty which establishes the formal border with Chinese Xinjiang, further dividing ethnic groups such as the Kyrgyz, Kazakhs and Uighurs.

1864 Russians capture Chımkent.

1891 Some million Russian migrants move into Kazakhstan.

1905 Alash Orda, the Kazakh nationalist party created.

1916 Major anti-Russian revolt by the Kazakh-Kyrgyz tribes. Several hundred thousand migrate to China.

1917 Alash Orda sets up independent government.

1918 June Kazakh Autonomous Region reestablished with Orenberg as its capital

1920 Alash Orda joins Bolsheviks.

1920 26 August The Kyrgyz Autonomous Soviet Socialist Republic is set up within the RSFSR.

1925 May: Kazakh Autonomous Province, ethnically correct name given to Kyrgyz Autonomous Province.

1928 First of many purges of Kazakh nationalists from CPKZ.

1930-31 Forced collectivization of Kazakh-Kyrgyz nomads. Tens of thousands killed or migrate.

1936 5 December: The Kazakh Soviet Socialist Republic is founded.

1940 Change over from Latin to Cyrillic for Kazakh, Kirgyz. Tajik Turkmen and Uzbek.

1941 Ethnic groups from Russia sent to Kazakhstan by Stalin.

1954 February: Virgin Lands Scheme begins. One million migrants from other republics arrive.

1964-86 Dinmukhamed Kunayev is first secretary of CPKZ.

1977 Third USSR constitution is adopted.

1986 1 December: Alma Ata riots begin after Kunayev is removed from of office and replaced by a Russian,Gennady Kolbin, Seventeen people are killed and hundreds are injured as riots spread to twelve other towns.

1989 28 February: Nevada-Semipalatinsk movement founded. June Nursultan Nazarbayev becomes first secretary of the

CPKZ.

1990 12 January: Radbek Nisanbai becomes grand mufti of Kazakhstan as new Islamic Religious Board is set up.

February 22: Nazarbayev is re-elected as first secretary and Chairman of the Supreme Soviet.

March USSR Supreme Soviet amends the 1977 Constitution create a new post of executive President Communists with Ninety four percent (330 out of 360 seats) in Kazakhstan.

APPENDIX - 3

CHRONOLOGY

1902. Rumours, reach the Viceroy of India, Lord Curzon, that the Russians have signed a secret treaty with the Tibetans. Preparations begin for a British military invasion of Tibet.

1903-4 Colonel Francis Young Husband marches with 3,000 British troops to Gyantse. The 13th Dalai Lama flees from their approach and shelters in Mongolia and in China. The British withdraw after signing the Anglo-Tibetan Convention which allows them to have trade agents at Gyantse and at Gartok in Western Tibet.

1909. The Dalai Lama returns from exile, Chinese troops occupy parts of Kham (Eastern Tibet) and the Dalai Lama appeals to Britain for assistance.

1910. A Chinese army, led by Zhao Erfeng (Chao-Erh-feng), invades Tibet and enters Lhasa. The Dalai Lama flees to India.

1911 In Beijing the Manchu (Qing) Dynasty is overthrown and the Republic of China is established under Yuan Shikai (Yuan Shihk'ai), who declares Tibet, Xinjiang (East Turkestan) and Mongolia to be provinces of China.

1912. Throughout the country Tibetans rise up against the Chinese.

August 12 The Chinese sign a Surrender Agreement with the Tibetans, and are obliged to return to China via India.

1913. The Dalai Lama returns to Lhasa and issues a formal Proclamation of Independence in conjuction with Mongolia.

1914. Tibet, Britain and China attend the Simal Convention as equal powers and initial an agreement, never ratified by China, to settle the Sino-Tibetan border dispute.

1918. Tibetan troops advance to the east and defeat the Chinese; the Treaty of Fongbatsa is brokered by Eric Teichman.

1920. Sir Charles Bell is set to Lehsa as British representative to reassure the Tibetans of British support for its self-rule and self-defence.

1923. The Panchen Lama, long distrusted for his close relations with the Chinese, disputes his tax liability to the Tibetan Government and flees to China.

1933. Choekyi Gyaltsen, the 13th Dalai Lama, dies in Lhasa aged 58.

1937. The 6th Panchen Lama (9th by the Chinese count)dies in jyekundo (Chinese: Yushu) on the Chinese border.

1940. Tenzin Gyatso, the 14th Dalai Lama, enthroned at Lhasa.

1941-4. Tibet remains neutral during the Second World War and refuses permission for the Americans or the Chinese nationalists to transport military supplies through Tibetan territory.

1947. Tibet sends a delegation to discuss trade and to open formal relations abroad, to India, China, Britain and America.

Tibet is nearly plunged into civil war when Retring, the former regent, supported by the monks of Sera, attempts a *coup d'etat.*

1949. In China the People's Liberation Army overcomes the Nationalists (KMT) and on October 1 Mao Zedhong proclaims the People's Republic of China. The 10th Panchen Lama, then eleven years old, telegram Mao Zedong asking him to 'unify the motherland'. The PLA announces its intention to `liberate Tibet from foreign imperialists'.

1950. The 14th Dalai Lama, then fifteen years old,takes over the running of the Government.

October 7, The Chinese cross the upper Yangtse River into Eastern Tibet and destroy for small garrison force at Chamdo in Khan. The Tibetan Government and the Dali Lama move to yarlung and send appeals for help to the United Nations. The British and the Indian delegates there persuade the General Assembly not to discuss the matter.

1951, May 23. The Tibetans, led by Ngapo Ngawang Jigme, sign the Seventeen Point Agreement with the Chinese, which promises cultural and political autonomy to Tibet but relinquishes independence. **October 24,** The agreement is ratified by the Dalai Lama and the National Assembly.

1954, April 29. India and China sign a treaty enunciating the 'five Principles of Peaceful co-existence', and recognising China;s claim to Tibet.

Revolt grows in Easter Tibet when the Chinese begin destroying monasteries and imposing collectivisation. Birth of the Tibetan resistance movement and of the Voluntary National Defence Army.

December 25. The Chinese declare open the Qinghai-Tibet and the Xikang-Tibet highways.

1955. Preparatory Committee for the Tibet Autonomous Region (PCART) set up with the Dalai Lama as chairman and the Panchen Lama and Zhang Guohua as deputy Chairman.

1956. The Dalai Lama goes to India for the Buddhas Jayanti celebrations and tells Nehru he wants to stay after Zhou Enlai and Mao promise that there will be no forced reforms, he returns to Lhasa.

1959, March 10. Thousands of Tibetans take to the streets in Lhasa. **March 17.** The Dalai Lama flees to India; 80,000 Tibetans follow him. **March 19.** Tibetan troops join the uprising against the Chinese. **March 23**. Uprising suppressed. The Chinese dissolve the Tibetan local government and impose a military government, fronted by the Panchen Lama, and in April begin 'democratic reforms'. Thousands of Tibetans are executed, imprisoned or sent to labour camps. Destruction of monasteries in Central Tibet begins.

1959-61. The Great Leap Forward leads to widespread famine, with up to 30 million believed to have died in China and many thousands in Tibet. Oxford University Press, 1994, p.xiii).

APPENDIX -4

Results of 1994 Parliamentary Election in Kazakhstan

Distribution of Seats by Oblast.

Oblast	No.of Seats
Aktubinsk	8
Almaty	9
Guryev (now Atyrau)	6
Mengistau	4
Zhambyl	10
Kzyl-Orda	6
Chimkent (now South Kazakhstan)	15
Almaty Alma-Ata (Capital)	15
Toldy-Kurgan	8
East Kazakhstan	10
Kokshetau	7
Parlodar	8
North Kazakhstan	7
Semipalatinsk	9
Ural'sk (now West Kazakhstan)	7
Tselinograd (now Akmola)	9
Karaganda	13
Zhezkazgan	6
Leninsk	3
Kustanay	11

Source: *Summary of World Broadcasts,* 19 March,1994.

SELECT BIBLIOGRAPHY

Primary Sources

(a) *Tibetan Sources*

Zwa-SGAB-PA DGAN-PHYUG BDE-LDAN BOD-KYI SRID-DON RGYAL-RABS (Kalimpong, 1976).

SITU PANCHEN CHOS-KYI 'BYUN-GNAAS and BELO TSHE-DBAN KUN-KYAB' *SGRUB BRUGYUD KARMA KAM TSHAN BRGYUDPA RIN-PO-CHEI RNAMPR THARPA RABSKYI (GYUN GNAS NOR BU ZLA BA CHU SAL GYI PHREN BA.*(New Delhi, 1972.)

STAG-LHA PHUN-TSHOGS BKRA-SIS, RGYA'I YIGTSAN NAN GSAL BA BOD KYI RGYAL RABS GSAL BA'I ME LON. (DHARAMSALA, 1973).

TA-LAI BLAMA (XIV), NOS KYI YUL DAN NOS KYI MIMAN (Darjeeling, 1983).

DRA-BO GTSUG-LAB PHREN-BA,*CHOS-BYUN MKHAS-PAI DGA-STON,* (Beijing,1986).

KUN-BZAN DPAL-JOR, *BSREGSKYAN MI-(TSHIGS PA;I BOD,*(Dharamsala, 1971

DUN-DKAR BLD-BZAN 'PHREN-LAS,BOD-KYI CHOS-SRID ZUN-BRAL SKOR BSHAD-PA (Bejing 1981).

BU-STON RIN-CHEN GRUB,*BU-STON CHOS-BUN (Chendu, 1988).*

(b) Russian Sources

Lykholata, Anderi, V., Natsionalizm-Vrag Trudiaschikhsia: Analiz Istoricheskogo Opyuta Bor' By Protiv Natsionalisma (Moscow:

Mysl; 1986).

Markhinin, Vasili, V.Osnovnya Zakonomernosti Protsessa internationalizatsii obschestvennoi zhizni Novosibirk; Nauka, 1989.

Materialy Vneocherednogo Plenuma Tsentral Nogo Komiteta KPSS,II Marta 1985 (Moscow, Gosizpolitizdat, 1985).

Mexhnatsional ' Nye Konflikty V Strane I Problema Obespecheniia Obshchestvennogo Poriadka, USSR Academy of Sciences Ministry of the Interior of the USSR (1990)

Otnoshene K.Russkim V.Soivzhykh Respublikakh, All Union Center for Public Opinion Research on Socio-economic issues, (Moscow 1991).

Sviridenko, IU.P, *Istorigrafita Leninskoi Nationnal 'noi Politiki (1960-1980gg)* Moscow, 1985.

Tsamerian, Ivan, P.Natsional 'Nye Ot Noshe NIA V SSR, (Moscow: Mysl 1987).

Zimanov, Salyk, Z, and Reiotor, Ivak. K. Teoreticheskie Voprosy Sovetskogo Natsional 'No-Gosudarstvennogo Stori Tel' STVA, (ALMA-ATA, NAUKA, 1987).

(c) *Sources in Translation*

Current Digest of Soviet Press (1986-1991), OHIO, USA.

Foreign Broadcast Information Service (Washington).

Summary of World Broadcasts Part I USSR, 1986-1991, BBC Monitoring Service (Caversham, Park Reading).

Secondary Sources

(a) *Theoretical Literature*

Books

Brass, Paul, R., *Ethnicity and Nationalism: Theory and*

Comparision (New Delhi: Sage Publications 1991).

Hall, Stuart, 'The Question of Cutural Identity' in Stuart Hall, David, Held and Tony M C Green, ed., *Modernity and its Futures,* (Oxford, UK: Blackwell Publishers, 1992).

Horowitz, Donald, L., *Ethnic Groups in Conflict: Theories, Patterns Policies* (Berkeley and Los Angeles: Univ. of California Press, 1985).

Kellas, James G., *The Politics of Nationalism and Ethnicity,* (New York: St. Martin Press, 1991).

Norbu, Dawa, *Culture and the Politic of Third World Nationalism.* (London: Routledge, 1992).

Phadnis, Urmila, *Ethnicity and Nation-Building in South Asia* (New Delhi: Sage Publication 1990).

Schermerhorn, R.A., *Comparative Ethnic Relations,* (New York: Randam House, 1970).

Shibutani, Tamotsu and Kwan, Kian *Ethnic Stratification: A Comparative Approach,* (New York: MacMillan 1965).

Walker Connor, *The National Question in Marxist-Lenist Theory and Strategy,* (New Jersey: Princeton, 1984).

Articles

Comaroff, John, L., "Humanity, Ethnity, Nationality: Conceptual and Perseptual and Comparative Perspectives on the USSR. *Theory and Scoeity,* (Netherlands, (20), 1991.

Walker Connor, "The Politics of Ethnonationalism", *Journal of International Affairs,* (New York), 27 (1), 1973.

Lapidius, Gail W., "Ethno nationalism and Political Stability: The Soviet Case", *World Politics,* (Dalles Texas), vol. 36 n.4, (1983-84).

General Books and Articles

A Scholar's Guide to Humanities and Social Sciences in the Soviet Successor States, Compiled by INION, Russian Academy of Sciences, Moscow and the Kennan Institute, Washington, D.C., M.E.Sharpe New York 1992.

Ad Shead, S.A.M. *Central Asia in World History,* (London MacMillan, 1993).

Addy, Premen, *Tibet on the Imperial Chessboard: the making of British Policy towards Lhasa 1989-1925).* (Calcutta, New Delhi, Academic Publications, 1984).

Ahmad Rashid, *The Resurgence of Central Asia: Islam or Nationalism,* (London, Zed Books, 1994).

Allworth, Edward, ed., *The Nationalities Question in Soviet Central Asia* (New York, Preager, 1973).

Anthony, Jones, et.al ed., *Soviet Social Problems* (Boulder CO, Westview 1991).

Avedon, J.F., *Tibet Today: Current Conditions and Projects,* Special Report Series 2 (The U.S. Tibet Committee, New York).

Azreal, Jeremy, R., *Soviet Nationalities Policies and Practices* (New York, Praegar Publication 1978).

Baker, Donald G., *Race, Ethnicity and Power: A Comparative Study,* (London, Routledge and Kegan Paul, 1983).

Barnett Robert and Akiner, Shirin, *Resistance and Reform in Tibet,* (London Hurst and Company, 1994).

Bell, Charles, *Tibet Past and Present* (London Oxford University Press, 1968).

Birch, Anthony, H., *Nationalism and National Integration*, (London Unwin Hyman, 1989).

Black, Cyri, E., et.al., *the Modernization of Inner Asia,* (New York, M.E.Sharpe, 1991).

Bowie and Fair Bank *Communist China 1955-59, Policy Documents with Analysis* (Cambridge, Massechuests, 1962)

Brandt, Conrad, Schwartz Benjamin, and Fairbank, John K., *A Documentary History of Chinese Communism* (London George Allen & Unwin Ltd., 1952).

Buttino, Marco, Feltrinelli, Fondazione, G., (ed), *In a Collapsing Empire: Under development, Ethnic Conflicts and Nationlisms in the Soviet Union,* (Milano, Italy).

Carrere D' Encausse, Helene, *Islam and the Russian Empire: Reform and Revolution in Central Asia* (London: I.B. Tauris, 1988).

China's Minority Nationalities, (Beijing, Great Wall Books, Published by China Reconstructs, 1984).

Coakley, John, *Territorial Management of Ethnic Conflict,* Frank Cass, 1993).

Collected Documents on Nationality Policy, (Beijing Peoples Publishing House, 1953).

Denber, Rachel, ed., *The Soviet Nationlity Reader: The Disintegration in Context,* (Boulder, CO, Westview Press, 1992).

Dick, Wilson., *A Quarter of Mankind: An Anatonmy of China Today,* (Harmondsworth, Penguin Books, 1966).

Dienes, Leslie, *Soviet Asia: Economic Development and nationality policy Choices.* (Boulder, CO, Westview Press, 1987).

Donnet, Pierre-Antoine, *Tibet: Surrival in Question,* (Delhi, Oxford Uiversity Press, 1994).

Dreyer, June Teufel, *China's Forty Millions,* (Cambridge, Harvard, 1976).

Eberhard, Wolform, *China's Minorities Yesterday and today,* Wadsworth, CA, Belmount, 1982).

Economic Review: Kazakhstan (Washington, D.C.: International Monetary Found, May 1992).

Eklof Ben, *Soviet, Briefing: Gorbachev and the Reform Period* (Bo'ılder, Westview Press, 1989).

Ellinwood, Dewitt, C, and Enloe Cynthia H. Ed., *Ethnicity and Militancy in Asia,* (New Brunswick: Transadian Books, 1981).

Fairbank, John, K. *The Cambridge History of China,* (Cambridge University Press, 1987).

Fieman, Wiliam ed., *Soviet Central Asia: The Failed Transition* (Boulder Co, Oxford University Press, 1992).

Freedom of Religion in China, Asia Watch and Tibetan Information Network (New York and Washington, Human Rights Watch 1992).

Geraed Cheliand, (ed), *Minority people in the Age of Nation-States,* (Delhi, Ajanta Publications 1990).

Gitelman, Zvi Ed., *The Politics of Nationality and the Erosion of the USSR,* Papers from the IV world Congress for Soviet and East European Studies, (Basingstoke and London, St. Martin Press, 1990)

Gleason, Gregory, *Federalism and Nationlism: The Struggle for Republican Rights in the USSR,* (Boulder, 1990).

Glebov, Oleg and Crowfoot, John *The Soviet Empire: Its Nations Speak Out* (London, Harwood Academic Publishers, 1989).

Goldstein, Melvin, C., *A History of Modern Tibet 1913-1951: The Demise of the Lamaist State,* (Berkely C.A., University of California Press, 1989).

Grunfeld, Tom, A., *The Making of Modern Tibet,* (Armonk, New York M.E. Sharpe, 1987).

Hajda, Lubmyr and Beissinger Mark ed. *The Nationalitieis Factor in Soviet Politics and Society,* (Boulder, Westview Press, 1990).

Herber, Thomas, *China and its Nationmal Minorities: Autonomy or Assimilation?* (New York, Armonk M.E.Sharpe, 1989).

Hiro, Dilip, *Between Marx and Muhammed, The Changing Face of Central Asia* (London Harper Colins Publishers, 1994).

Hosking Geoffery, *The Awakening of the Soviet Union,* (Cambidge, M.A. Harward University Press, 1991).

Information China: The Comprehensive and Authoritative Reference Source of New China, vol.3 The Chinese Academy of Social Sciences (Oxford, 1989).

Karem Padayumane P., *The Changing Face of Tibet: The Impact of Communist Ideology on the Landscape,* (Lexington, University of Kentucky Press, 1976).

Klieger, Christiaan, P., *Tibetan Nationlism the role of Patronage in the Accomplishment of a National Identity,* (Meerut, Archana Publications, 1992).

Kort, Michael, *The Soviet Colossus; The Rise and Fall of the USSR,* Armonk, M.E. Sharpe, New York.

Lacquer, Walter, *Soviet Union 2000: Return or Revolution* (London, I.B. Tauris, 1990).

Lane, David, *State and Politics in the USSR,* (Oxford, UK, Basil Blackwell, 1985).

Lapidus, Gail, Zaslovsky Victor, Ed. with Philip Goldman, *From Union to Common Wealth Nationalism and Separatism in the Soviet Republics,* (New York, cambrige university Press, 1992).

Lewis, Robert, A., *Geographic Perspectives on Soviet Central Asia* (New York, Routledge,1992).

Liberthal, et.al, ed., *Perspectives on Modern China* (New York M.E. Sharpe Inc, 1991).

Mac Farquhar, Roderick, ed., *The Politics of China* 1949-1989, (New York, Cambridge University Press, 1993).

Mackerras Colin *Minorities: Integration and China's Modernization in the Twentieth Century* (Hongkong, Oxford University Press, 1994).

Ming, Yin, *United and Equal: progress of China's Minority Nationalities* (Peking: Foreign Language Press, 1977).

Mosley, George, *The Consolidation of the South China Frontier,* (Berkeley, University of California Press, 1973).

Mosley, George ed. and tr. *The Party and the National Question in China* (Cambridge, Mass: MIT Press, 1966).

Motyl, Alexander J.ed. *Thinking Theoretically about Soviet Nationalities: History and Comparision of the Study of the USSR,* (New York, Studies of the Harriman Institution, Columbia University Press, 1992).

Nahaylo, Bohdan and Swoboda, Victor *Soviet Disunion* (New York: The Free Press, 1989).

National Minorities, Questions and Answers about Chinese, (Beijing Foreign Language Press, 1985).

Naumkin, Vitaly Panarin and Sergeif ed., *State Religion and Society in Central Asia.* (England Ithaca Press, Reading).

Nove Alec, *An Economic History of the USSR (1917-1991).* London, Penguin, 1993).

Paksoy, H.B. (ed),*Central Asia Reader: The Rediscovery of History,*

(New York, Armonk, M.E., History, 1992.

Parsons, Sir Authony, *Central Asia Reader : The Last Decolonization,* The David Davies Memorial Institute of International Studies (London Occasional Paper, no.4 August 1993.

Pipes, Richard, *The Formation of the Soviet Union Communism and Nationalism* (1917-1923), Cambridge Harvard University Press, 1984.

Poliakov, Sergei P.ed., *Everyday Islam: Religion and Tradition in Rural Central Asia* (New York Armonk, M.E.Sharpei, 1992).

Ra'anan, Uri, and others ed. *State and Nationin Multi-Ethnic Societies: The Breakup of Multinational States* (New York, Manchester University Press, 1991).

Richardson (Hugh E.) *Tibet and its History* (Boulder Co. Shambhala, 1984).

Roi, Yaacov ed., *The USSR and the Muslim World* (London Allen and Unwin, 1984),

Rothman, Jay, *From Confrontation to Co-operation Resolving Ethnic and Regional Conflict* (London Sage, 1992).

Rumer, Boris ed., *Soviet Central Asia: A Tragic Experiment* (Boston, Unwin Hyman, 1989).

Rupesinghe Kumar, King Peter, Vorkunova Olga, ed., *Ethnicity and Conflict in a Post-Communist World the Soviet Union, Eastern Europe and China* (New York, St. Martin Press Inc., 1992).,

Rywkin, Michael, *Moscow's Muslim Challenge - Soviet Central Asia* (London: C. Hurst & Co., 1982).

Schwarz Henry G., *Chinese Policies Toward Minorities: An Essay and Documents* (Bellingham, Western Washington

State Collage, 1971).

Seton-Watson, Hugh, *Nations and States, An Enquiry into the Origins of Nations and the Politics of Nationalism* (London Methuen, 1977).

Shakabpa, Tsepon W.d., *Tibet A Political History* (New York: potala Publications 1984).

Sharma, Swarn Lata, *Tibet: Self-Determination in Politics Among Nations* (New Delhi, Criterion Publications, 1988).

Simon, Gerhard, *Nationalism, and Policy Toward the Nationalities in the Soviet Union: from Totalitarian Dictatorship to post-Stalinist Society,* (Boulder, Westview Press, 1991).

Simpson, G.E. and Yinger, J.M., *Racial and Cultural Minorities: An Analysis of Prejudice and Discrimination* (New York, Harper and Routledge, 1992).

Singh, K.S.ed. *Ethnicity, Caste and People* Proceedings of the Indo-Soviet Seminar held in Calcutta and Leningrad, 1990, (Anthropoligical Survey of India, New Delhi, Institute of Ethnography Moscow, Manohar, Publishers. 1992).

Skockpol, Theoda, *States and Social Revolution: A Comparative Analysis Of France,* Russia and China (Cambridge, Oxford University Press, 1979).

Snellgrove, David and Richardson Hugh, *E.A Cultural History of Tibet* (Boston and London, Shambala, 1986).

Stavenhagen, Rodolfo, *The Ethnic Question Conflicts, Development and Human Rights* (Tokyo, United Nations University Prss. 1990).

Tibet Under Chinese Communist Rule: A Compilation of Refugee Statements 1958-75 (New Delhi Information and Publicity Office of H.H. Dalai Lama, 1976).

Vaidyanath, R., *The Formation of Soviet Central Asian Republics* (A Study Soviet Nationality Policy) (1917-30) (New Delhi, People's Publishing House, 1967).

Van Walt, Van Praag. *Tibet and the Right to Self-determination* (Dharmasala, Information Office, Central Tibetan Secretriat, 1979).

Van Walt Van Praag (Michael.C), *The Status of Tibet: History, Rights and Prospects in International Law,* (Boulder Co., Westview, 1987).

Walkerr, Lee and Sterm, Paul (ed.), *Balancing and Sharing Power in Multi-ethnic Societies* (Washington, National Academy Press, 1993).

Wang Xiaooqiang and Bai Nanfena, *The Poverty of Plenty* (London, Macmillion 1991).

Warikoo, K. and Norbu, Dawa, *Ethnicity and Politics in Central Asia* (New Delhi South Asian Publishers Pvt. Ltd., 1992).

Wheeler, Geoffrey. *The Modern History of Soviet Central Asia* (New York, Praeger 1964).

White, Stephen, Pravada, Alex and Gitelman Zvi ed., *Development in Soviet and Post Soviet Politics* (North Corolina, Duke University Press).

Wimbush S.Enders, *Soviet Nationalities in Strategic Perspetive* (London Crom Helm, 1985).

Wirsing, Robert ed., *Protection of Ethnic Minorities: Comparative Perspectives* (New York, Pergamon Press, 1981).

Yuan-Li-Wu, Ta-hing Lee et.al., *Human Rights in the People Republic of China* (London, Boulder Co. 1988).

Articles

'A Sea of Troubles', Special Report on Nationalism, Tumoil and change in the CIs, *Strategic Digest,* (New Delhi), Vol. XXIV no. 2, Feb 1994.

Ahmed S.H."China and Tibet,1949-1959", *International Studies,* (New Delhi), Vol.10.no.4, April 1969.

Anderson Barbora A, "Muslim Riots in Alma-Ata", *Arabia,* vol. 6, no.66, Feb, 1987.

Bahl, S.K., China's Failures in Tibet: Pulls and pressures of Domestic Politics, *China Report* 25 (3) July-Sept 1989, (259-90).

Basilov, V.N., 'Popular Islam in Central Asia and Kazakhstan', *Journal Institute of Muslim Minority Affairs.* (London), 8(1) Jan 87, 7-17.

Bhutani V.C. 'Tibetan Aspirations', *China Report* (New Delhi), 23 (3) July-Sept 87 34-17.

Bray,John, 'China and Tibet An End to Empire? *World Today* (London), 46(12), December 1990, 221-24.

Brezinski, Zbgniew, 'Post-Communist Nationlism', *Foreign Affairs,* (New York), vol.68, no,5,1989-90.

Brown, Bess, 'The Public Ror in Prestroika' *Central Asian Survey,* (London), vol. 9, no.3, 1990.

Broxup. Marie, "Islam in Central Asia since Gorbachev" *Asian Affairs,,* vol. XVIII, part III, Oct. 1987.

CCP Polity on Minority Nationalities (Nov - 6 1938), Document, *(Chinese Law and Government,* (New York), vol. XIV, no. 4, 1981-82.

Cockburns, Patrick, 'Date line USSR: Ethnic Tremors' *Foreign Policy,* 74, Spring; 1989, 168-84.

Conolly Violet, 'Interpretations of Soviet Policy Towards Central Asia and Siberia' *Asian Affairs,* (London), 17(1), February 1986, 69-72.

Deglopper, Donlad R. 'Chinese Nationality Policy and the Tibetan Question', *Problems of Communism,* (Washington), 39 (6) Nov-Dec 1990; 81-89.

Delf, Robert, "A loss Horizon" FEER, vol. 139, no. 17 March 1989, p. 24.

Dienes, Leslie: Regional Planning and the Development of Soviet Asia, *Soviet Geography,* (Columbia) May 87, 287-314.

Dreyer, June Teufel, "China's Quest for a Socialist Solution", *Problem of Communism,* (Washington), vol.24. no.5. September-October 1975, p.49.

———, "China's Minority Nationalities in the Cultural Revolution" *China Quarterly,* (London), no.35. July-Sept.1968.

———,'Unrest in Tibet' *Current History* (Philadelphia), 88 (539) September 1989, 281-84.

Dunlop, John B, 'Will the Russians Return from the near Abroad'. *Post-Soviet Geography,* vol.35. no.4. April 1994.

Ernest Raiklin, *The Deintegration of the Soviet Union,* vol.28, 3/4, 1993, Oxford.

'Events in Kazakhstan: A Eyewitness Report', *Central Asian Survey,* (London), 6(3), 1987, 73-76.

Fireman, William 'Religion and Nationalism in Soviet Central Asia', *Problems of Communism,* (Washington), 38(4) July-August 89 (123-27).

Gleason, Gregory, 'Political Elite in the Muslim Republics of Soviet Central Asia the Dual Criterion of Power, *Journal Institute of Muslim Minority Affairs.* 10(1) Jan. 1989, pp.246-63.

———, 'Nationalism and its Discontents', *Russian Review,* (Cambridge), vol. 52, no. 1, January 1993, p. 79-90.

———, 'Independent Muslim Republics in Central Asia: Legacy of the Past, Shape of the Future', *Journal Institute of Muslim Minority Affairs* (London), 12(2) July, 1991.

———, 'Political Elite in the Muslim Republics of Soviet Central Asia: The Dual Criterion of Power' *Journal Institute of Muslim Minority Affairs* (London), 10(1) Jan 1989, 246-63.

———, 'Independent Muslim Republics in Central Asia: Legacy of the Past, Shape of the Future, *Journal Institute of Muslim Minority Affairs,* (London), 12(2) July, 1991.

Granberg, A.G., "Economic Relations Among the Republics: Forms and Essential Features" *Soviet Anthropology and Archelogy* 26(3) Winter 1987, pp.77-96.

Greene, Felix, 'True History of Sovereignty' *Third World Unity,* Oct-Nov, 1978, 29-32.

Grunfeld, A. Tom, 'In Search of Equality: Relations Between China's Ethnic Minorities and the Majority Han' *Bulletin of Concerned Asian Scholars.* (Boulder CO.), January 1985, vol. 17, no. 1, p. 54-67.

Harris, Chauncy D., 'Ethnic Tensions in the Successor Republics' Post-Soviet Geography, (Columbia), vol. 35, no. 4, April 1994.

Hecher Michael, Lev Margaret The Comparative Analysis of Ethno-Regional Movements, *Ethnic and Racial Studies,* (London), vol. 2, no. 3.

Hinton Harold,'National Minorities in China', *FEER,* (Hongkong), Sept. 15, 1955, vol. 19, no. 11, pp. 321-327.

Horowitz Donold, 'Ethnic Separatism', *Comparative Studies in*

Society and History, (London), vol. 23, no. 2.

Hunter, T. Shireen, 'Nationalist movements in Soviet Asia' *Current History,* (Philadelphia), vol. 89, no. 549, Oct. 1990.

Isinaliyev, mikhail, 'Diplomacy of Kazakhstan', *International Affairs* (London), (4), April 89, 51-58.

Issacs, Harold R., 'Nationality, End of the Road', *Foreign Affairs,* (New York), April 1975, pp. 432-447.

Jigmi, Ngapoi Ngawany, "Great-Changes in Tibet", *China Today,* (Beijing), May 5, 1991, vol. 40, no.5, pp. 8-12.

Jisi, Guo, 'China Promotes Human Rights: Religious Freedom', *Beijin Review,* Jan. 28-Feb. 3, 1991, vol. 34, no. 4, pp. 15-16.

Kaiser, Robert and China Jelf 'Russian-Kazakh Relations in Kazakhstan', *Post-Soviet Geography,* (Columbia), vol. 36, no. 5, May 1995.

Kazakh and Russians close on Nationalities issues in Kazakhstan', *Opinion Research Memorandum,* U.S. Information Agency, (Washington D.C., March 19, 1993).

Khan R. 'Central Asia's Geo-Political Importance', *World Focus,* (New Delhi), Nov-Dec. 1992.

Koroteeva V. and Others, "From Bureaucratic Centralism to Economic Integration of sovereign Republics", *Problems of Economics,* 32(3), July 1989 (36-58).

Lafitte (Gabriel), "Opportunities for a new era in Tibetan-Chinese Relations", p. 1, *Tibetan Review,* (New Delhi), 24(11), Nov. 89, (11-4) pt. 4, Dec. 89 (14-7).

Lapidius, Gail W., "Ethno-Nationalism and Political Stability: The Soviet Case", *World Politics,* (Dallas, Texas), vol. 36, no. 4, 1983-84.

Lieven, Dominic, 'Gorbachev and Nationalities', *Conflict Studies*

(London), Centre for Security and Conflict Studies, Nov. 1988.

Malik, Iftikar, 'Issues in Contemporary South and Central Asian Politics: Islam, Ethnicity and the State', *Asian survey,* (London), Oct. 1992.

Mao Tse Tung, 'On Coalition government', *Selected Works,* vol. IV (Peking, Foreign Languages press, 1967).

Mehapatra, Uma Kant, "Tibet-Grouping Towards a Solution", *China Report,* (New Delhi), vol. 24, no. 3, July-Sept. 1988.

Mehra, Parshotam, 'Tibet on the Imperial Chess Board: A Select Bibliographical Survey 1924-1984', *India Past and Present* (Bombay), 3(2), 1986, 253-70.

Minority Areas, *Beijing Review,* May 13-19, 1991.

Mirsky, George I., "Central Asia's Emergence, *Current History,* Philadelphia), 91(567), Oct. 1992, pp. 334-38.

Misdaq, Nabi, 'Central Asia Waking up to its Past', *Writers Union of Free Afghanistan* 6(1), Jan-Feb. 91: 31-39.

Modak, Ashok. "Soviet Muslim Policy", *Political Science Review,* (Jaipur), Jan-June 1986.

Mosley, George, 'China's Fresh Approach to the National Minority Question', *The China Quarterly,* (London), Oct-Dec. 1965, pp. 15-27.

Mosley George, 'The Frontier Regions is China's Recent International Politics", In Jack Gray ed., *Modern China's Search for a Political Form* (London: Oxford University Press, 1969).

Motyl Alexander J., 'The sobering of Gorbachev: Nationality Restructuring and the West', in Seweryn Bialer ed., *Politics Society and Nationality* (Boulder, 1989).

Naitow wu, 'Lamaism flourshing in Tibet', *Beijing Review,* Oct.

26, Nov. 1987, pp. 23-26.

National Minorities, *China New Analyses,* (Hongkong), no. 720, Aug 9, 1968.

National Minorities, *China New Analyses,* no. 831, Feb. 12, 1971.

National Minorities, *China New Analyses,* no. 909, Feb. 9, 1973.

Nationalism and National Attitudes on the Eve of the Coup Series of Articles, *sociological Research,* (New York), Nov-Dec. 1992, vol. 31, no. 6.

Norbu, Dawa, 'Chinese Communist Views on National Self Determination, 1926-56: Origins of China's Minority Policy', *International Studies* (New Delhi), Oct-Dec. 1988.

– ——, 'Chinese Strategic thinking on Tibet and the Himalayan Region,, *Strategic Analysis,* (New Delhi), 12(4), July 88, 371-395.

———, 'C, 'Ninteen-Fifty-Nine Rebellion: An Interpretation'. *China Quarterly* (London), (77) March 1979, 74-93.

———, 'Ch, The Tibetan Response to Chinese Liberation, *Asian Affairs,* vol. 62, no. 3, 1975, p. 27.

Norbu Dawa 1991, "China's with the Dalai Lama 1978-90: Prenegoliation Stage or Dead End", *Pacific Affairs,* (Canada), 64(3), pp. 351-72.

Norbu Jamyong, Tibetan Perspective on China after Deng Xiaoping, *Tibetan Review,* 26(6), June'91.

Olcott, Martha Brill, 'Central Asia's Post-empire Politics', *Orbis* (Philadephia), 36(2), Spring 1992.

———, 'Ch' 'Central Asian Catapult to Independence'. *Foreign Affairs* (New York), 71(3) 1992, 108-30.

Ostapenkolly, and Susokolov (A.A.), Inter-regional Mixing and the National Composition of Labor Resources, *Soviet Anthropology and Archaeology,* 26(3), Winter 1987, pp. 61-76.

Patterson, Mervyn Soviet Central Asia: A Time for Reflection, *Middle East International* (Washington), (434), 25 Sept. 92, pp. 18-19.

Peter William, 'Central Asia and the Minority Question', *Asian Affairs* (London), 22(2) June 1991, 152-57.

Pipes, Richard 'The Soviet Union Adrift', *Foreign Affairs,* (New York), vol. 70, no. 1, 1991.

Prag, Michael Van Walt, "The Changia World Perception of the Tibetan Situation", *Tibetan Review,* Sept. 1991, pp. 11-13.

'Public Role in Perestroika', *Central Asian Survey,* 9(1) 1990.

Qing Zhou, Yu Xiong, 'Population Growth of Minority Nationality' *Chinese Sociology and Anthropology,* (New York), no. 3-4, vol. XVI, 1984, p. 192.

Raeder, Philips, G., 'Varieties of Post-Soviet Authoritarian Regimes", Philip, G. Raeder, p. 66, 73, 78 etc. *Post-soviet Affairs,* (Columbia), vol. 10, Jan.-March 1994.

Rakowka Harmstone, T., 'The Dialects of Nationalism in the USSR', *Problems of Communism,* vol. 23, May-June 1974.

———, 'C, Teresa. "Readings on Soviet Multinationalism", *Soviet Anthropology and Archeology,* (New York), vol. 26, no. 3, Winter 1987.

Roi, Yaccov, 'Islam and Nationalism in Soviet Central Asia', *Problems of Communism* (Washington) July-August, 1990.

Rongxia, Li, "Potala Palace under Overall Revolution", *Beijing Review,* Feb. 11-17, 1991, vol. 34, no.6, pp. 19-23.

Rywkin, Michael. "Religion, Modernization, Nationalization,

Nationalism and Political power in Soviet Central Asia", *Canadian Slavonic Papers,* (Los Angeles), vol. XVIII, no. 2-3, summer Fall 1975.

Schopflin, George 'Nationalism and National Minorities', *Journal of International Affairs,* New York, vol. 45, no. 1, Summer 1991, pp. 51-65.

Segal Bernard E., 'Ethnicity where the Present is Past' in R.L. Hall (ed.), *Ethnic Autonomy Comparative Dynamics* (New York, 1979).

Sharma (RR), "Class and Social Agrarian Transformation in Soviet Central Asia: A Historical-Cultural Context", *Man and Development* (Chandigarh), 8(3), Sept. 86, pp. 112-27.

Shorish, M.Mobin. "Dissent of Muslims, Soviet Central Asia in the 1980s", *Nationalities Papers,* (Oxon, England), vol. 9, no. 2, Fall, 1981.

Singh Gurman, 'Modernization, Ethnic Upmrge and Conflict in the World', *International Journal of Group Tensions* (New York), vol. 24, no. 4, Winter 1994.

Smith Anthony d., 'Ethnic Identity and World Order', *Millenium,* (London), vol. 12, no. 2.

Stads, David R., "Minorities of Inner Asia", *Problems of Communism* (Washington D.C.) vol. 27, May-June 1978.

"Stobdan, Dynamics of Central Asia", *Mainstream* (New Delhi), 29(51), 12 Oct. 1991.

Stoddard, Heather, 'Tibet from Buddhism to Communism', *Government and Opposition,* (London), 21(1), Winter 86, pp. 76-95.

Taras, Kuzio, 'Nationalist Riots in Kazakhstan' *Central Asian Survey,* vol. 7, no. 4, pp. 79-100.

Tianlu, Zhang, "Growth of China's Minority Population", *Beijing Review,* June 18, 1984, vol. 27, no. 25, pp. 26-30.

Tibet, *China Report* (New Delhi), 24(3) July-Sept 88 213-394,

Series of Articles.

Tibet launches massive Project, *Beijing Review,* Jan. 21-27, 1991, vol. 34, no. 3, p. 6.

Tibet's Case for Self-determination: H.H. The Dalai Lama of Tibet? *Strategic Digest,* (New Delhi), 21(5), May'91, pp. 957-62.

Tibet-China Report 24(3), July-Sept. '88, pp. 213-394, Sage Pubs (Series of Articles), New Delhi.

Ulmasov A., Sharifkhodzaev, "Formation and Development of Socialist Economy in the Central Asian Republics", *Problems of Economic* 28(6), Oct. 85, p. 74-86.

Van Valt Van Praag (Michael C.) "Changing World Perception of the Tibetan Situation", *Tibetan Review,* 26(9), pp. 11-13, September 1991.

Van Valt Van Praag, Michael C., 'Publication Transfer and the Survival of the Tibetan Identity', *Strategic Digest* 18(1), Jan 88, 35-50.

Vasukic V.B. 'Popular Islam in Central Asia and Kazakhstan', *Journal Institute of Muslim Minority Affairs,* 8(1) Jan 87, 7-17.

Vonojzeng Li "Education Among Minority Peoples', *Beijing Review,* Oct 17, vol. 23, no. 42, pp. 16-23.

Voskressenski, Alexei D., "Current Concept of Sino-Russian Relations and Frontier Problems in Russia and China", *CAS* (1994), 13(3), pp. 361-381.

Vujacic Velijiko and Zaslavsky, Victor, 'The Causes of Disintegration in the USSR and Yugoslavia', *Telos,* (New York), no. 88, Summer 1991, pp. 120-140.

Wangcherk Sharlo, Tsetan, 1992, 'China's Reforms in Tibet: Issues and Dilemmas', *Journal of Contemporary China*

1(1), pp. 34-60.

Warikoo, K. 'Central Asian Resurgence' *Seminar* (New Delhi), no. 393, May 1992, p. 30-33.

Wimbush Enders, S. "The Muslim Ferment in Soviet Central Asia", *Global Affairs* (Washington), vol. 11, no. 3, Summer 87.

Wixman, (Ronald). "Demographic trends among Soviet Muslims. 1959-79. *Soviet Geography,* 2(1) Jan. 84".

Xingwu, Liu and Alatan, Liu, "China's Policy Towards Her Minority Nationalities", *Social Scientist* (New Delhi), vol. 16, no. 1, Jan. 1988.

Yannian, Pai, "Helping Tibet Train its People", *Beijing Review,* Oct. 19, 198, vol. 30, no. 42, pp. 4-5.

Yannian, Pai, "Helping Tibet Train its People", *Beijing Review,* Oct. 19, 1987.

Yavuz, M. Hakan, "The Patterns of Political Islamic Identify: Dynamics of National and Translational Localities and Identities", *Central Asian Survey* (London), vol. 14, no. 3, 1995.

Zeki Velidi, Togan, "The Current Situation of Muslims in Russia", *Central Asian Survey,* vol. 8, no. 2, 1990.

Zheng Zhou, "Visit to Tibet: Modernization in a Buddhist Land", *Beijing Review,* Aug. 26, 1985, vol. 28, no. 34, pp 15-23.

Zhou Zheng, "Modernization in a Buddhist Land", *Beijing Review,* 28 (34), Aug. 26, 85, pp. 15-23.

Zwarycz, Roman, "Critical Re-examination of Gorbachev's Reform Programme from the Prespective of National Liberation Struggle", *Ukranian Review,* 28(34), Summer, 1990.

News Papers

Financial Times	(London)
International Herald Tribune	(New York)
Kazakhstanya Pravda	(Alma-Ata)
Los Angeles Times	(New York)
New York Times	(New York)
People's Daily	(Beijing)
Pravda	(Moscow)
The Guardian	(London)
The Hindu	(New Delhi)
The Hindustan Times	(New Delhi)
The Independent	(London)
The Observer	(London)
The Statesmen	(New Delhi)
The Times	(London)
The Times of India	(New Delhi)
The Tribune	(Chandigarh)
The Wall Street Journal	(London)
The Washington Post	(London)

Press Release and New Agencies

New China New Agency	(Beijing).
Novosti, Press Agency	(Moscow).